T0149956

Casino Gambling

Casino Gambling

Play Like a Pro
in 10 Minutes or Less!

Frank Scoblete

Chicago and Los Angeles

07 06 05 04 03   5 4 3 2 1

Library of Congress Cataloging-in-Publication Data

Scoblete, Frank.
  Casino gambling : play like a pro in 10 minutes or less! / Frank
Scoblete.—1st ed.
      p. cm.
Includes index.
  ISBN 1-56625-199-0
1. Gambling. 2. Casinos. I. Title.

  GV1301.S385 2003
  795—dc22

                                    2003019163

Bonus Books
875 North Michigan Avenue
Suite 1416
Chicago, Illinois 60611

Printed in the United States of America

In memory of

Dorothy Campion
Mary Moscariello
Robert Quattrocchi

Table of Contents

Chapter 1

The Count of Three

What is the leisure activity in which more adult Americans participate than any other? Going to movies? Playing softball? Golf? Bowling? Come on! Tennis? Oh, my aching elbows! Stamp collecting? Coin collecting? You're getting colder. Quilting? Sure, it is big with the truckers. Reading great literature? Ha! Ha! Ice cold. Freezing.

More than 53 million Americans participated in this activity last year; plus, millions of Canadians, Mexicans, and just about every nation's citizens around the world participated, too. People with money. People without money. Yes, Virginia, I even saw a guy in a Santa Claus suit doing it last Christmas.

It is gambling.

From kitchen poker games to sports and horse betting, to dogs and dominoes, more people gamble than do just about anything else other than eat, sleep, work, and make more people. And the biggest draw in the world of gambling is unquestionably casino gambling. Las Vegas has gone from a sleepy little desert town to a sprawling metropolis. Atlantic City has been resurrected. Tiny delta counties such as Tunica have become giant pools of money. Riverboats ply the waves up and down the Midwest. And Indian casinos are changing the concept of the word "reservation" from a holding area for an oppressed people to, "Will that be a deluxe room or a suite, sir?"

The Purpose of This Book

This book has three goals:

1. To give you easy-to-learn, mathematically superior strategies that can be mastered in *10 minutes or less* so that you can go to a casino tonight and play with confidence
2. To help you manage your money and your mind so that you get the most from your casino experience
3. To acquaint you with the great tales, legends, history, and lore of casino gambling

Why This Casino Gambling Book Is Better Than the Others

Timothy James Connors, age 17, has a tendency to deviate from the norm by at least three standard deviations both physically and psychologically, and he fluctuates from probability in his behavior based on the parameters of his peer group's behavioral patterns.

Now, if that sentence sounds a little too formal, bloodless, or weird, you are right—it is! Why? Because it was written in math- or science-speak and, as such, conveyed very little useful information about Timothy to a general audience; that is, an audience composed of you and me and people who actually communicate using language.

So, in English, here is that first sentence again, conveying a lot more information, albeit colored by my loathing of Timothy James Connors: *My friend's son, Little Timmy (also known as Terrible Timmy), is a hell-raising, nasty, violent, out-of-control 17-year-old 5'2" nutcase who probably will wind up in jail for his disgustingly criminal activities by the time I finish this sentence.*

Now, the difference between sentence number one and sentence number two is that the former is clinical and contains no overt advice, but the latter lets you know, in no uncertain terms, that (1) Little Timmy is trouble, (2) Little Timmy is dangerous, and (3) Little Timmy should be avoided.

The reality of the world at large—and Little Timmy in particular—is not fully served by a math-science description of behavior or of the workings of the natural world. After all, the taste of chocolate and the feeling of love that you have for your spouse are not the same thing, even if the same pleasure centers of the brain are activated. While a chemical formula might create or encourage a feeling, it is not the feeling in and of itself. It isn't the reality. It is merely a cold, bloodless description. Nor, indeed, is reality fully served by an emotionally packed, real-world description teeming with judgmental adjectives, as in my sentence about Little Timmy. In fact, to get a handle on the world at large—or Little Timmy in particular—it is necessary to run the gamut from supposedly objective observations and formulas to completely subjective ones. And then, for good measure, one should confront the world at large—or Little Timmy in particular—head on and experience the thing for oneself. In short, chocolate tastes a lot better on the tongue than it does on the page.

You might be asking yourself, what does Little Timmy's description have to do with casino gambling? My answer is short: everything.

If you read even the best books on casino gambling that are written from the bloodless math-science perspective, you may never understand that the math is warning you. When you gamble, there will be some nights when you, a fully grown, supposedly mature, responsible person, will feel like crawling into a crib and sucking your thumb until you fall asleep. It can be *that* bad. Instead, the books will say that your results have deviated from the mean by X number of standard deviations—but go tell that to your thumb, which is now blistering from all that sucking.

Of course, highly personalized and thoroughly suspect idiosyncratic real-world accounts of why playing a particular author's way is guaranteed to bring home millions of dollars of casino lucre will also lead to thumbsucking and a concomitant desire to sic Little Timmy on said author of such tome. Few of the idiosyncratic authors take the time to warn their readers that their strategies can, and do, fail at times (or in the long run), so be wary when playing them.

In truth, the casino gaming experience is really two experiences and their subsets. The first is clinical, bloodless, and intellectual; the second is subjective and supercharged with emotions:

1. The strategy you employ at the games, including your gambling system and money management
2. The adventure of the games, including the thrill of winning money and the tall tales and lore of the games

This book will give you a very good understanding of both experiences in quick, easy, and fun chapters.

Strategy

Gambling systems generally boil down to a few types. These can be systems based on the following:

1. The *mathematically best bet,* which gives the house the least possible edge at the game or gives the player the edge
2. *Data* such as basic strategies for card games based on computer simulations and mathematical analyses; card

counting or trends (the type of data can be fact or fancy, the point is that the player bases decisions on it)

3. *Systems* that exploit the physical weaknesses of a game, such as rhythmic rolling in craps or biased wheel play in roulette

Adventure

One of the reasons for playing in a casino is the sheer thrill of it, the adventure of it all. Every casino player has war stories of the night everything went heavenly or everything went to hell. We have all met the *ploppies* of gambling: the compulsives and the completely clueless. Play in a casino for any length of time, and personal stories abound. But only a few casino players know about the rich lore in casino gambling of those truly epic wins, those larger-than-life characters, those amazing streaks, and those bizarre occurrences. Indeed, as every country and culture has its legends and myths, so too does casino gambling. A part of the thrill of playing in a casino is knowing that you are stepping onto a battlefield that has seen greatness. Truly savvy casino players play against the backdrop of history, which makes it just that much more fun.

How Much Do You Really Need to Know to Be a Good Player?

Recall when former President Clinton was caught with his pants down, metaphorically speaking, and he equivocated with the now-famous quote: "It depends on what the definition of 'is' is." Well, "good," when it comes to players in casino games, has a number of definitions. Some gambling purists will die trumpeting the idea that no player can be good if he is playing a *negative-expectation game* (i.e., a game where the casino has an edge). By this definition, the only good players are those who have an edge over the house. Others take the opposite approach: because casino players are playing for fun, it does not matter how they play. Thus, every player is a good player. The casinos love this particular definition, but they add another wrinkle to it: *and the more money they play, the better!*

I take a more moderate view. I think people have a tendency to gravitate to games that intrigue them, regardless of whether it is possible to get an edge or not. A good player, once he has settled on his game of choice, develops a strategy aimed at reducing the house edge and the hourly rate of expected loss. A good player tries to get the most comps for the least play. A good player is in control of his emotions and never bets more than he intends to bet. By my definition, there are good slot players, good video poker players, good roulette players, good craps players, good Let It Ride players, even good Sic Bo players, and so on. Based on my definition, a good player will not necessarily be able to beat the casino in the long run, but will not just throw his money down the tubes, either. Indeed, in casino gambling, as in life, there are better ways to play the game.

So how much do you really need to know to be a good player at casino games? In some games, not much. In others, a little bit more. In still others, quite a lot. In poker, for example, there is no such thing as a good losing player. Like a prize fighter, *winning* determines worth at poker, because a poker player does not play against the house. At slots, on the other hand, knowing the right machines to play and how to play them (one coin, full coin, tortoise, or hare-like) are the only strategic criteria. So, at slots, what you need to know to be good *tonight* is not very daunting.

Of course, if you take a look at some casino gambling books, you will see incredibly complex mathematical formulas for determining this or that strategy. If this is the first casino book you have ever read, do not panic! Just as someone does not need to know the physics of a combustion engine to drive a car, you do not need to understand the complex mathematical calculations underlying casino games to play well. The recommended strategies derived from these calculations are often as easy as (1) turning the key in the ignition, (2) putting the car in drive, and (3) stepping on the gas. This book concerns itself with getting you from point A to point B, not with looking under the hood.

The games are divided into three categories:

1. Simple games requiring few strategy choices (slots, roulette, casino war, three-card poker)
2. Moderate games requiring simple strategic decisions for good play (Let It Ride, Caribbean Stud, Pai Gow Poker, craps)
3. Complex games requiring more than a handful of strategic decisions for good play (blackjack, video poker)

In no case will the strategies given in this book require you to spend more than 10 minutes learning them.

So how good can such easy strategies be? Very good to excellent. In some games, such as blackjack, the difference between my ten-minutes-or-less basic strategy and the full-blown basic strategy is about 0.5 percent. That is very good. In Caribbean Stud, the difference between my ten-minutes-or-less strategy and the most complex strategy is in the tenths-of-one-percent range. That is excellent. Always keep in mind that I am discussing casino gambling strategies in this book, not brain surgery. Most games are relatively simple to learn, simple to play poorly, and almost as simple to play well. So why not play well? A good bet is just as much fun to make as a bad bet—in fact, it is more exciting to make a good bet because you are more likely to win.

Are the strategies in this book the best possible strategies for the games discussed? Some are. Some are not. In games where the strategy is not the best possible strategy, I will point you in the direction of how to get even better ones. However, the effort required to master, say, blackjack card counting and other *advantage-play techniques* (i.e., techniques that give you an edge over the casino) is much greater than the average casino player wishes to exert. The extra effort, once the game is mastered, increases in inverse proportion to the benefits gained by such effort. Taking blackjack as an example again, my 13-part strategy will see you playing against an approximate 1 percent house edge, instead of the 2 percent to 5 percent edge most other players face. That is some significant reduction. However, if you decide to learn the correct basic strategy for the play of every hand you get against every dealer up-card, it will take several days (at a minimum) to master. The attendant reduction in the house edge will be approximately another 0.5 to 0.75 of a percent; instead of facing approximately 1 percent of the house edge, you will face approximately 0.25 to 0.5 percent of the house edge. Is it worth it to learn more complicated strategies? In most cases, no. In some cases, the answer is yes. (I made it easy to use the full basic strategy by putting it in a chart form. You can photocopy it and bring to the casino.)

Of course, if you already know your way around the games, this book still might appeal to you because it has stories and anecdotes, legends and lore, that will interest, intrigue, and amaze you—some published for the very first time. I also tackle some issues that all gamblers face, such as whether to bet with or against trends, how to establish a bankroll, and, most importantly, how to get the most comps as possible.

Hopefully when you finish this book, your appetite will be whetted for more learning, deeper insights, and stronger—though more demanding—strategies. To this end, I recommend further sources for your inquiring mind at the end of chapters and in the appendix of the book. There is a wealth of books and tapes on all aspects of casino gambling available to the savvy player. The player who stops learning starts losing.

Chapter 2

General Gambling Principles

What you will read in this chapter applies to all casino games in which the house has an edge over you. And what is an "edge"? Simply, the percentage of all the money you wager that the casino expects you to lose. So, if the house has an edge of 5 percent on you, for every $100 you bet, you can expect to lose $5 in the long run.

Principle 1:
The Casino Edge Means
When You Win, You Lose!

When I first started my gaming career, my mother took me aside and said: "Be careful. The casinos will win in the end." I asked her why and she replied: "Because the casinos are the casinos."

Now, she didn't know about odds and edges, speed and number of decisions; she knew one thing: "The casinos will win in the end." I pressed her further. Did she think nobody ever won? Did everybody walk away a loser every day and every night? "No," she said, "people win, but then they lose. They win, but then they lose."

Without fully understanding the math behind her statement, my mother had cut to the quick of why casinos win in the long run and why almost all players lose in the long run. It is a very simple concept really: the casinos win when the players lose, of course, but *the casinos also win when the players win!*

There is nothing diabolical about this, as you shall see, and it works like this:

Games are structured in two ways to give the casino the edge. The casino can win more decisions than the player, or the casino can *tax* the player's winning bets. In craps, for every 495 Pass Line decisions, a Pass Line player will win 244 decisions but will lose 251 decisions, on average. That seven-decision shortfall on the part of the player means the casino has a 1.41 percent edge on the game. (Just divide 495 into 7 and you get 0.0141414.) That means, for every $100 bet, you should expect to lose $1.41 in the long run. As house edges go, this is, comparatively, quite low. So the Pass Line bet would be considered a good bet to make.

If we take a look at the worst bet on the craps table, the Big Red or Any 7 bet, we see how the casino utilizes a *tax* to generate profits. In 36 rolls of two six-sided dice, the 7 will come up six times on average. That's because the 7 can be made in six different ways (1:6; 6:1; 2:5; 5:2; 3:4; 4:3). The probability of getting a 7 on any given roll is therefore 6 in 36, or one in six. That means for every 7 that shows, five non-7s will also show. That makes the odds on the 7 appearing five to one. In a "fair game," defined as a game where nobody has an edge, a winning Any 7 bet would pay $5 for every winning $1 wagered. The player would lose $5 on the five $1 bets he lost, win $5 on the one bet he won, and everybody goes home even (in the long run).

Unfortunately for the player, the casino cannot make any money on the Any 7 bet if it pays off at five to one. So when you bet the Big Red or Any 7, the casino does not pay you the true odds of the bet. Instead it pays you four to one. So you lose five times ($5), and win once ($4), and you are down a dollar. In a very real sense, the casino keeps that extra dollar for itself! So, when you win, you also lose.

In roulette, we see the same kind of tax being imposed. On the American double-zero wheel, there are 38 pockets for the ball to fall into: the numbers 1 through 36 and the 0 and 00. The probability of any individual pocket hitting is 1 in 38. The odds of winning are therefore 37 to 1. The casino pays out $35 for every winning $1 bet, in essence keeping $2 for itself. That becomes the casino edge on roulette, 5.26 percent. (Just divide 38 into 2 and you get 0.0526315.) Again, when you win, you lose.

Card games can be much more complicated to analyze than other games because the number of possible card combinations is enormous. However, blackjack falls into the first category of games—the casino wins more decisions. Approximately 48 percent of the decisions are won by the casino, 44 percent by the player, and 8 percent are ties (I have made these even numbers so they are easier to remember). So how is it that blackjack is such a close game? Because on those 44 player wins, the casino will sometimes pay more than even money (a blackjack), or it will allow the player to increase his bet in player-favorable situations (doubling down and splitting pairs). That makes up some of the shortfall the players face. But it isn't enough to make the game a positive one for players using basic strategy (0.5 percent) or my ten-minutes-or-less strategy (1 percent).

Now, students of business should not be shocked that the casinos attempt to structure their games so that they have the edge. After all, no one is shocked to learn that the local department store actually makes a profit on you when you buy your cookware, or that your local bookstore marks up its books, or that your local supermarket has the audacity to profit from your hunger by charging you more for the food than it costs them. When you buy a television set, you don't think you are getting it for what it really cost to build.

For businesses to function, they must make profits. That is a no-brainer.

Sadly, some other no-brainers of the human variety, in a misguided effort to keep the rest of us from having fun, often articulate the notion that somehow or other it is immoral for the casinos to charge a tax on their games, or to structure their games so that they win more decisions from the players than they lose, in order to guarantee a profit for their owners and investors. Why is that immoral? Business is business. The casinos are not interested in gambling on their own games; they want the math on their side. By analogy, what is the sense of making a new product if you sell it for less than what it costs to make? The casinos sell their games to the players, and it is up to the players to get the best bargain they can, just as it is up to shoppers to be cost-conscious when they make a purchase. In some rare cases, such as card counting at blackjack and controlled shooting at craps, the skilled player actually can flip the edge to himself.

Overall, however, my mother was right when she said: "The casinos win in the end," because if they did not, there would not be any casinos at all—and where would that leave all of us casino-thrill shoppers? There are only limited thrills to be had at Home Depot, after all.

When shopping for casino edges, the lower the better. However, the edge of a casino game is not the sole criteria in judging whether this or that game or strategy is the one for you. Another ingredient is just as important: speed!

Principle 2:
Better to Run into a Wall Slowly

Let us do a little mind experiment. Two identical model cars starting from two hundred yards away from the same solid brick wall start to accelerate toward the wall. Car #1 gets up to 50 miles per hour before hitting the wall, while car #2 only gets to three miles per hour before hitting it. In which car would you rather be? Unless you have a death wish, the answer is obvious. Even though both cars traveled over the same length of road and hit the same wall, the speed of each was the determining factor in the difference between a crumpling crash and an itty-bitty bump. Of course, if you were a collision company, you would prefer car #1 because the damage done to it would make for a very good payday, a very good payday indeed.

In casino gambling, many players pick car #1 as their car of choice—to the delight of the casino "collision experts" who deftly persuade their customers to drive very fast into the wall called "house edge." And how is fast driving analogous to casino gambling? Simple. The faster you play, the more you will lose in the long run. This is easily demonstrated in another mind experiment.

Two identical $1 slot machines are standing side by side. They have the exact same payback structure, let's say 95 percent (which means for every $100 you play in the machine, it returns $95; or you can say that the casino has a 5 percent house edge, and the player can expect to lose $5 for every $100 wagered). On slot machine #1 is Mr. Hare, who plays $1 per spin, with a reel spin or decision every five seconds—or 12 decisions per minute, 720 decisions per hour. He puts through $720 per hour, and he can expect to lose $36 per hour playing this way. Next to him is Mr. Tortoise, who plays $1 every 15 seconds—or $4 per minute, 240 decisions per hour. He puts through $240, and he can expect to lose $12 per hour. Same machines, same paybacks, different speeds of play.

The number of decisions per hour is as important as the house edge. In fact, people who ignore the speed of the games they play are just asking for their bankrolls to crash, *kaboom*, into the wall. For all games where the casino has the edge, this dictum holds: *the slower you play, the better.* Determine in advance just how many decisions you are going to give yourself in an hour, and stick to it. At slot machines, this is easy to do because you control the pace completely—the machine dances to your rhythm. At card games, it is slightly more difficult.

Often dealers, especially at blackjack, want to impose their rhythms—which are often fast, faster, and even faster than that—on the players. Doing so can cause the players to make mistakes in their hitting, standing, doubling, and splitting strategies. A rushed blackjack player is a bad black-jack player.

If you are a basic strategy blackjack player, you should always *take your time* when deciding how a hand is to be played. The dealer can harrumph, stomp her foot, utter sar-castic remarks, or even attempt to play your hand for you—but she cannot pass you by until you make your decision. Never let a dealer impose her rhythm on you. And if you find that you are about to play more hands than you had deter-mined in a given hour, what should you do? Sit out some hands! By doing this, you are in control of the speed of the gambling car as it approaches the house-edge wall.

Principle 3
High-Return and Side Bets Are Usually Bad Bets

"Hey, it's only a buck. One little, tiny, itsy-bitsy buck," said the man. "And I have a shot at some big money, too. There's very little real risk now, is there?"

Although the rationale for playing the slot machines is often this very sentiment, the chance at winning a lot with a lit-tle investment, the above fellow was not a slot player; he was a table-game player. And he was commenting on his penchant for making "Crazy Crapper" proposition bets in craps and for always and invariably making those jackpot side bets in Caribbean Stud, Let It Ride, and, when available, in blackjack.

When I mentioned to him that on many Crazy Crapper bets the casino has double-digit edges and that those jackpot side bets can come in with 20 to 30 percent edges, he looked at me as if I were from another planet.

"Yeah, so? So what?"

"Those are mighty big edges to try to overcome," I repeated.

"But they are only on a stinking dollar. Big deal. A 30 percent edge on one dollar is a measly 30 cents. I can live with that."

I attempted to explain to him that he was looking at the situation in a very narrow fashion, as a *single* bet, and that he should look at the big picture: a truckload of bets. But he was not interested in what I had to say. Recognizing this, I parted company with him, as I do not think it is judicious to give advice to folks who do not really want it, despite the fact that I am in the casino-gambling-advice business.

I will readily admit that the man was right about one thing. On a single one-dollar bet with a high house edge—such as the Any 7 at craps that comes in with a 16.67 percent casino edge—what is a measly 16 or 17 cents? Who cares, indeed? Some people do not even bother to pick up a penny or a nickel or a dime if they see it on the floor, so the prospect of losing such denominations on a given bet is no big deal.

And the casinos *bank* on that attitude when offering those wild, wacky, and wicked jackpot side bets for a "measly dollar" and all those Crazy Crapper proposition bets on the craps table. In fact, they bank on it in all high-return wagers, even if these wagers are only for a "measly buck." Why? Because no one makes just one $1 bet in his or her gambling career; instead, players make hundreds of them in a given night, thousands of them during a given casino vacation, and, perhaps, hundreds of thousands of them in a given casino gambling career. And boy do they add up—to nifty wins for the casinos and hefty losses for the players.

Let us take a look at a typical Crazy Crapper bet at craps, the "yo-eleven," a one-roll bet that the 11 will be the next number rolled. You bet one dollar on the 11 and, if you win, you win $15. However, the true odds would pay you $17. That two-dollar shortfall gives the bet an 11.11 percent house edge. (Is that mystic or what? The yo-eleven, which means 11:11, has a house edge that is 11.11 percent? Numerologists, please note!)

So, for every one dollar you bet on the 11, you will lose 11 cents in the long run, which is not such an awesome prospect on one bet. But what about the fellow who makes that bet on every come-out roll? Or on every shooter? Or, heaven forbid, on every roll? He could be throwing that yo-eleven bet on the layout anywhere from 25 to 150 times per hour! At 11 cents a pop, the long-run losses can add up. a given hour sees him lose between $2.75 to $16.50; a four-hour session (the minimum for full comps) could get pricey at $11 to $181.50. Now, what if he were visiting the casinos for five days and playing four hours per day? A loss of between $55 and $907.50 looms.

The yo-eleven is not even the worst of the Crazy Crapper bets, just the most esoteric. You could go really crazy and bet the Any 7, the 2 or 12, and find your money dribbling away at an even faster rate over time. Keep in mind that a life-time of Crazy Crapper bets, even for a measly dollar a pop, will add up to a bankroll-sucking vampire. For those of you who make these bets for even larger sums, as many players do, then you are begging to be taken to the cleaners, and you'll get starched by them all right.

Now, the one-dollar jackpot side bets that you find at Let It Ride, Caribbean Stud, and, occasionally, at blackjack are just as awful: most come in with between 20 and 30 percent edges. If we take a 25 percent edge as an average and postu-late that these games see 60 to 90 decisions per hour, you can see that a one-dollar side bet is $60 to $90 per hour wagered into the gaping jaws of that 25 percent house edge. You'll lose between $15 and $22.50 *per hour!*

A $5.00 blackjack player playing my ten-minutes-or-less strategy in a multiple-deck game can expect to lose a mere $4.50 per hour at 90 decisions per hour—which would be a very fast pace. But if this same individual springs for that one-dollar side bet, he could find himself losing five times as much!

So, yes, one bet for a measly dollar is no big deal, no matter how high the house edge. But when you add that bet up over time, that one dollar grows and grows—and so will your losses. Remember this: the biggest, fiercest snowstorm is just one measly flake piled upon another measly flake upon another measly flake . . . until you cannot see your lawn, your bushes, your trees, or your way.

So, the rule for high-return bets and side bets is very simple: never make them!

To recap:

1. The house gets its edge by winning more decisions or by taking a tax out of player wins.
2. Fast speeds are bad.
3. Avoid high-return and jackpot side bets.

Chapter 3

Playing the Games

Let me tell you two quick stories:

A friend of mine was in an African country teaching at a local college. He was new to the college, new to the country, but he decided to take a trip into the countryside to check out the local wildlife. His car broke down about 20 miles out of town, and he decided to hitch a ride. After several minutes, a car came down the dusty road, and he stuck his thumb out to hitch.

The car screeched to a halt. My friend figured, "What a friendly country this is. The very first car stopped!" But then the driver and three male passengers got out and proceeded to pummel my friend almost into unconsciousness and left him lying in the dust by the side of the road. Once he could get his mind together, and long after the car with the attackers had driven off, my friend dusted himself off and waited for the next car. It soon appeared. Again, he stuck his thumb out. *Screeeech!* The second car slammed to a standstill and again the driver got out. My friend figured he was dead as this driver was a towering, muscular specimen of a man, and he was coming right toward him. "No, no, no," said the man-mountain in a pleasant lilt, "you will get killed. You do not ask for a ride by insulting the driver's family."

Then the friendly native informed my friend that in his country, the American hitching sign was tantamount to saying that the driver's mother was having sex with a baboon or other lowly animal. It was the highest of insults. He went on to explain that to hitch a ride, you hit the back of one hand against the palm of another because "you are begging for a ride."

Had it not been for that nice mountain of a man, my friend might never have survived his roadside situation. He was in another country, and he didn't understand the culture of that country.

In a similar vein, another friend of mine was teaching at a local high school. A girl, just recently arrived from China, was placed in my friend's homeroom class. My friend gave her the schedule of classes she would follow, but at the end of homeroom she came up to him and was clearly upset. In broken English she said: "Can't go to that class! No! No!" She pointed to the biology class on her schedule. My friend tried to figure out why the thought of going to biology was such a scary proposition for the girl. Finally, after much effort, the girl said she could not go "to that fucking class." My friend was shocked at the language coming from this seemingly genteel young lady. Then the girl added that the class "sucks."

It took him a while to realize what had happened. The girl had very limited English. When she had gotten her schedule, another student took a look at it and helpfully informed her that he "hated that fucking class" and that as far as he was concerned "it sucks." She took his words literally and was shocked to discover that in America we had a "fucking" class where we also taught oral sex techniques! Needless to say, it took a little doing to explain to her that in America there were no literal "fucking" classes and that "sucks" was just a word that American teenagers used to mean something wasn't good. This poor girl was in another country and its slang had confused her.

Well, the casino is like another country; it has its own rules, language, and culture. Each table game is like a province in a country, with its own distinct dialects and mores. To not feel like an unwanted foreigner, you have to understand the language and culture—and then you must assimilate. The casino is Lady Luck's melting pot. And there is only one way to do things when in a casino—the casino's way!

The Buy-In

Before you can play any casino table game, you have to exchange your cash for chips. Here certain rules apply. Never hand your money directly to the dealer. She is not allowed to take anything directly from the hands of a player. In fact, a dealer is not even allowed to *shake* the hands of a player! You must put your money on the layout.

The dealer will take the money on the layout and spread it for the camera and the floorperson to check. The *floorperson* is the man or woman not in uniform who oversees several tables in a pit. A *pit* is a group of tables, usually of the same game, in a given area of the casino. The person in charge of a pit is a *pit boss.*

Once the floorperson okays the amount of the buy-in, the dealer then takes chips out of her chip tray, counts out stacks equal to the buy-in, and stuffs the cash into a hole in the table, where it is collected in a drop-box. Again, the floorperson checks to make sure that the dealer has counted everything out correctly. When the dealer gets the nod, she slides the stacks of chips to the player, usually saying, "Good luck."

The casinos are sticklers for the proper buy-in procedures. They have to be. The most frequent source of theft in a casino is from the casino's own personnel. Often, such theft is in collusion with a player, either a friend or a relative of the dealer. By making the physical contact between dealer and player verboten, it reduces the possibility of, say, the player announcing he is buying in for a $100, getting $100 worth of chips and, in fact, only giving the dealer a $10 bill that is quickly stuffed into the drop-box.

Of course, even with all the proper procedures in place, cheating dealers sometimes can be so ingenious they are able to rip off their employers anyway. I saw a video, presented at a security seminar, where a dealer was able to shovel chips directly into her sleeve as she counted or collected chips. Once she had several chips up her sleeve, she would then raise her arm slightly and the chips would go down into her shirt. If you were not told what to look for, you never would have seen the move—it was that fast! In the past, dealers have shoveled chips into their pants (usually they would have a sock in their crotches that would hold the chips), and their mouths, and some dealers have even "accidentally" (but fast) dropped chips that their player-henchmen would later "find" on the floor. You will note that many casinos now have dealers wearing shirts with sleeves that cling tightly to the wrists and aprons that surround their pants or dresses.

Betting Procedures

Casino chips come in all sorts of denominations and colors. Usually, $1 chip are white (sometimes blue); $5 chips are red; $25 chips are green; $100 chips are black; $500 chips are purple; $1,000 chips are gold or grey, and $2,000 chips are orange. It's rare to see denominations larger than $2,000, except in some high-roller rooms. The sizes of the chips vary as well. The $1 to $500 chips are the same size, but, usually, the $1,000 and higher denominations are somewhat larger.

Once you have your chips, you can begin to bet. However, even here there are certain protocols that must be followed. When you are betting different denominations of chips, you must place the highest denomination on the bottom and go up accordingly. So if you want to bet $131, you would put a black chip on the bottom, a green chip on top of that, a red chip on the green chip, and a white chip on the red chip. With the exception of roulette, all casino table games within the same casino use the same denominations and colors. Because individual bets from a variety of players are stacked next to and upon one another, roulette games have many different colored chips, the denominations of which are determined by the player. When a player buys in at roulette, he states the value of his particular colored chips. Although a player can bet the normal casino chips at roulette, he can usually do so if he is the only one betting accordingly.

Each individual game will have certain protocols as well. These I will discuss as they come up. Suffice it to say that if you want to know how to hitch a ride, or if you are trying to figure out the nature of the class you are taking, it is always best to ask first, before you get yourself upset or into hot water.

Chapter 4
The Easy Games

Slot Machines

The industrial revolution of the late 1700s and early 1800s saw machines displace man in the manufacturing of just about everything, except perhaps other human beings. In 1811 in England, organized retaliatory groups of angry workers, both those who were employed and those who were unemployed, known as Luddites, went around smashing machines and decrying the fact that man was being replaced by soulless, heartless, inhuman, almost Satanic, devices. The jobs those workers performed are long gone, as are those workers. The machines that took their place, that outperformed them, have birthed a world that looks to machines not only to do physical labor, but also to answer some of the most profound questions of science.

Apocryphally, the slot revolution of the 1970s in America saw one poor table-game dealer who had just been let go at the Landmark in Las Vegas take a sledgehammer to a machine on the casino floor and scream: "You son of a bitch! You're gonna kill all of us!" From our source (one of the most *unreliable* sources we have, unfortunately), this dealer, or rather *former dealer,* got in two hefty whacks with the sledge-hammer before he was carted off shrieking and foaming to Clark County jail. This poor dealer was worried that the machines were taking over the casino industry, and, indeed, he was right. Today, almost three-fourths of the casinos' profits are from the machines, and, in some areas of the country, close to 90 percent of the gross is from the pulling of handles and the pressing of buttons.

Although human dealers have not as yet been replaced by machines (in fact, there are more dealers today than ever before because of the explosion of casinos across America), the percentage of live gaming employees who deal directly with the games in the casinos has decreased in direct proportion to the increase in the number, scope, and variety of machines. This change has even hit, well, the making of change. Thus, the change people are being phased out by slot and video-poker machines that accept bills and make their own change. It makes you wonder if some casino Luddites just might be stockpiling sledgehammers.

And what has caused such consternation among the human casino workers? Why, the very things which have lured more people into casinos than to live athletic events in the past decade—those incredibly smart, incredibly charming, incredibly winning, computer-driven slot machines.

The Luddites are dead and buried. Their factories are now places where men service machines that do the yeoman's share of the work and create the royal share of the profit. So, too, in casinos. Slots are king. They are the mother lode of gold for the casinos. Even a superficial examination of the casino landscape will show this. For every billboard that extols a given table game or table-game option in the casinos, there are probably 10 or more that extol the wonder of the machines.

An alien from another planet, if he, she, or it were reading the ads in all the magazines and newspapers for casinos, would think the following: casinos are places where some famous humans sing or tell jokes or do magic or punch each other in the face, and where all the rest of the nonfamous humans go to play with "loose" or "hot" or "high-payback" machines with fanciful names. The alien, upon a close examination of the machines, would discover two very important facts. The first is that the machines are not really the lumbering, heavy pieces of mechanical equipment that at first they appear to be, but, rather, they are sophisticated, computer-controlled devices with programs that determine everything that will happen inside and outside them. While slot machines deal in chance, nothing inside the slots—either physically or in terms of the programming—has been left to chance. They are marvels of design, and the casinos can take the execution of that design to the bank—which of course they do.

Most slot players approach the machines with awe and respect for the potential gold mines contained therein. Yet many slot players have no idea of how the machines work or, worse, they have strange conceptions based on idiosyncratic experiences and shared mythologies. Make no mistake about it, as graveyards and old houses in every town across America have myths and legends about them, so too have the slot machines. When people do not know the facts, they allow myths to make the explanations.

Today's slot machines are programmed by computer to continually select a series of numbers at random, whether the machine is being played or not. The random-number generator, or RNG (some writers call this the pseudo-random-number generator), continually picks number series that correspond to the various symbols on the reels or to blank spaces. When a player puts in his coins and then either pulls the handle or presses the button, the computer spins the reels to tell the player which number series was "it" when that handle was pulled or that button was pushed or those coins went in.

Many players believe that the independent spinning of the reels is the selection principle. Sorry, no. In the old days, the reels operated independently and spun until they stopped. In the old days, no one could predict where the reels would stop. Today, the reels will stop where the computer tells them to stop—based on the number series that had been previously selected by the RNG for each reel. The reels have no independent action. They are being coordinated perfectly by the RNG and the computer. In fact, the spinning of the reels is merely a show, a diversion, an entertainment, as the reels could just as easily put up the symbols that have been selected immediately. Who knows, but in the future, as slot players become more attuned to the true nature of their machines, the spinning of the reels will become passé. Instead, you will put in your coin, press that button, and instead of waiting a few seconds for reels to spin, you will be told pronto whether you won or lost. The time saved by eliminating the spinning reels will reap the casinos riches far surpassing anything they have today.

Since the modern slot machine is programmed to select number series at random, no amount of finessing of the handle can change what has been decided; nor are there built-in win/loss cycles as some players believe. In any series of random events—and the selection of the number series by the RNG is considered a random event—all manner of bizarre patterns will develop. There will be machines so hot they will pay out for hours on end. Other machines will seem to be so cold that they could substitute for icemakers. Still others will seem to hit a few, cool off a little, hit a few, cool off a little and so on. Yet, when you look at the performance of these machines in a given year, you will note that most come in at— or extremely close to—their programming.

And how are they programmed? The casinos cannot make money if they return to the player more money than— or the same amount of money as—the player originally put in them. Instead, the machines return a *percentage* of the money put in them. Thus, if a machine is returning 92 percent, that means that in the long run of that particular machine's programming it will give back 92 cents for every dollar played. It keeps 8 cents on the dollar.

Now, people would not play slot machines if every time they put a dollar in they got 92 cents back. What fun would that be? You'd be better off playing the change machine—which is, after all, a 100 percent payback machine. Still, the change machine is rather dull. You put in a dollar; you get back a dollar. Where is the fun in that? Where is the adrenaline rush?

Instead, the slot machines are programmed to return their percentages explosively. That is, sometimes nothing comes out (more often than not), and sometimes a hell of a lot comes pouring out (rare, but heart-throbbingly exciting). It is the lure of a great windfall (or even a little breeze) that excites the slot player. After all, inside the bellies of some of those computerized beasts are sequences that can make you rich and richer and even richer than that—and the heart pounds with that knowledge. And thus the casino can return its 92 cents on the dollar because it is giving us more than eight cents worth of anticipatory thrills with every dollar we plunk into the machine's maw.

There is only one way to beat the slot machines that are programmed to return less than 100 percent of the money put in them (which is just about every slot machine on the face of the Earth), and that is to take a hammer, a great *BIG* hammer, bash the machine with all your might, crack open the money-holding area, put all those coins in a big bag or bucket, and then run like a deer for the exits and hope that the security guard following you is the one who was thinking of signing up for Weight Watchers next week. If not, you will not enjoy the peculiar slot games they play in prison.

So does that mean there are no strategies for playing the slots? Does it mean that you might as well walk into the casino, spin a bottle, and play the first machine it lands on—thereby kissing your money good-bye?

Not at all.

Even in negative-expectation games, and slot machines are a negative-expectation game (except to the casinos), there are better ways to play. Slot machines, as opposed to video poker machines, are not games of skill. The only decisions you make with the slots are the following:

1. Which machines to play
2. How many coins to play in them
3. When to stop playing

But these decisions are not to be considered frivolous and unimportant. Yes, in video poker, you will get to make discreet, individual decisions that will influence what the machine will return to you. Make the right decisions, and you'll get the highest payback the machine offers; make the wrong decisions, and you won't.

In slots, you cannot influence what the machine will do. You can just pick the machine that will do it to you.

So which machines are good and which are not? That is a matter of opinion and temperament. Are you looking to play a machine that returns a little a lot? If you are, you will play a machine that has many small pay lines and very few big ones, and you'll get many small payouts but not many big ones.

Or are you looking to make a killing and want to play machines that return a lot a little? Then you'll pick machines that have a few big pay lines but very few small ones. You will find that you'll not make many winning combinations, but the ones you do make will be for hefty sums.

Let us go over that again. On the "little a lot" machines, you will have a *high-hit frequency*. You will find that you win a little, lose a little, win a little, lose a little, and that you are often ahead of the game at any given point in your play. On these machines, you will find that after a *prolonged period* of play, you will be down "X" amount—"X" being in the vicinity of the machine's programming.

On the other hand, on the "a lot a little" machines, called *low-hit frequency* machines, you will find that spin after spin after spin are losers and then, *bam*, you'll get a nice hit for a substantial sum, sometimes enough to put you in the black, sometimes way in the black, and then . . . you will lose, lose, and lose some more. At the end of a *prolonged period* of play, you will find that you are down "X" amount—again "X" being in the vicinity of the machine's programming.

The above machines actually could be returning the exact amount, say 95 percent, of all the money put in them. So what is the difference?

On the high-hit-frequency machine, you won't have to bring as much money to the casinos on any given night because you can expect to see money coming out of the machine to help fuel your evening's play. On the low-hit-frequency machine, you'll need a much more substantial sum in order to weather the losing storms that inevitably will appear. It is possible, though not probable, that you could hit big early, but if you do not you will need some dough backing your play. In the end, both machines will take and pay out what they are programmed to take and pay out—they just take it and pay it differently.

Personally, I prefer to win "a little a lot" and not "a lot a little."

The second question concerns how many coins to play in your machine. Here again, it is a matter of opinion and temperament. If you play a machine that rewards the maximum coin, then it might be worth your while to play maximum coin. How much of a reward would be necessary to make playing full coin worth a player's while? Take a look at the jackpot line of a three-coin machine. If one coin wins 200, and two wins 400, and three wins 800, is it worthwhile playing three? The extra value is a mere 200 coins for playing the max. But to get that small return you have to risk three times as much money. It is not worth it.

However, if the max coin line goes something like this: 200, 400, 1,800, then the extra 1,200 coins might very well be worth your risk.

Again, I have my personal favorites in terms of coinage. I prefer to play machines that do not reward extra coin, machines that would go something like: 200, 400, and 600. There is no reason to play maximum coin in such a machine because maximum coin is merely a multiple of a single coin. In this case every coin is worth 200 on the jackpot line. You can play three spins of one coin to try to win 600 coins or you can play one spin of three coins. You will be able to play a lot longer if you decide to play one coin. You will s-t-r-e-t-c-h your pleasure, but not your risk!

The third and final question concerns when to stop. Obviously, if you've lost every penny you brought to gamble with, that might be a good time to leave. A better way to approach the question would be to say: "I want to play for four hours. How many spins will I make in those four hours, and how much will I need to make those spins?" Answer the questions and bring the exact amount you'll need to play exactly as you planned. Approached this way, it would be rare indeed to lose every penny you brought.

Although slot machines are programmed to return "X" amount, you can be the deciding factor in how that "X" amount is going to be returned to you.

The Ten-Minutes-or-Less Slot Machine Strategy

1. *Avoid all progressive machines such as Megabucks, Quartermania, etc.* These machines usually return between 83 and 89 percent of all the money played in them in order to generate the large jackpots, pay the licensing fees, etc. According to slot expert John Robison, author of *The Slot Expert's Guide to Playing Slots* (Huntington Press, $6.95), the odds of hitting a Megabucks jackpot are almost 50 million to one— worse than most state lotteries! (Okay, okay, if you must play them on occasion in order to dream those mega-jackpot dreams, then play full coin and only 10 percent of your gambling stake.)

2. *Play one coin in equal distribution machines.* Look for stand-alone machines, meaning machines that are not linked to other machines sharing the same jackpot, and that do not reward you for playing extra coins. The

Wild Cherry and Double Diamond are examples of such. Check the jackpot line and make sure that all payouts are merely the same multiples of the first coin (i.e., 1 coin = 300 coins; 2 coins = 600 coins; 3 coins = 900 coins). Also, see if you can find such machines being "certified" as guaranteeing a 97 or a 98 or, good luck, a 99 percent return. However, be careful of the signage. If it says "these machines return *up to* 98 percent, that means only one machine needs to be returning that percentage; the rest can be returning far less. You want each machine to be certified.

3. *Play machines that have a lot of little payouts, instead of a few big payouts.* These machines will usually give you the best chance of winning something, even a small something, on any given night because they are probably high-hit-frequency machines.

4. *Slow the pace.* Remember that speed kills bankrolls. Try to play one decision every 10 to 15 seconds. If a machine has a handle, pull the handle, as that automatically helps to slow the pace. Hey, you'll also get a little exercise!

5. *Adhere to the "rule of three" in managing your money.* Divide the money you are going to play within a given session into three equal parts. If you should lose one-third of it on a given machine, take a breather or switch machines. This will not increase your chances of winning, but it will allow you to get your composure back if, like me, you find that an extended losing streak is painful. Follow the same procedure with the second and third parts. Never allow yourself to lose all your money on one machine or on one prolonged session!

6. *Avoid those multi-line, nickel machines.* Without realizing it, many nickel players have become high rollers by betting upward of one, several, or many dollars per spin on small denomination machines that reward you for more coins with more pay lines and symbols. These machines do not pay back well at all—often returning

no more than 85 to 90 percent of all the money played in them. If you want to play $1 in a machine, you are much better off playing a single dollar in a dollar machine than 20 nickels in a nickel machine!

7. *Be leery of branded machines.* Machines that are based on television shows, movies, etc., will often be somewhat tighter than non-branded machines because the casino must pay the licensing fee for use of the copyrighted material.

8. *Always use your player's card when you play.* Do not play for comps, but take whatever the casino gives you for your play.

For More Information on Slot Machines

Break the One Armed Bandits: How to Come Out Ahead When You Play the Slots! by Frank Scoblete (Bonus Books, $9.95): The number one bestselling slots book of all time that has an exclusive interview with a casino slot executive who explains where the casinos place the "loose" and "tight" machines on their floors. Contains a complete history of the slot machine, plus valuable playing tips to reduce your risk and increase your chances of winning. Has an extensive section that shows which slot "facts" are facts and which are really myths and mistakes.

The Slot Expert's Guide to Playing Slots by John Robison (Huntington Press, $6.95): This small handbook contains valuable information on how the various machines are programmed and how to play them. Robison is known nationally as "the slot expert" and this book is a no-nonsense peek inside the machines.

Secrets of Modern Slot Playing by Larry Mak (L&M Publications, $9.95): Sensible slot strategies, including which machines to play and which to avoid. This is also a very humorous book with many insightful observations of the human condition.

Robbing the One-Armed Bandits! by Charles Lund (RGE Publishing, $14.95): There are rare times when slot machines "go positive." These are on some games that have a "bank" (such as Piggy Banking, Fort Knox, etc.). This book will explain what to look for on these sometimes-beatable games.

Roulette

There are two types of roulette wheels: the American double-zero wheel (you'll notice a green 0 and 00 opposite each other) and the European single-zero wheel (just one green 0). The casino has an edge of 5.26 percent on the double-zero wheel and an edge of 2.70 on the single-zero wheel. It achieves its edge by not paying back the true odds of the bet (see chapter 2).

The layout closest to the wheel has the green zero(es) at the peek, and then proceeds in three columns, with the number running across the columns. Thus, 1, 2, and 3 are at the top under the green zero(es); then under them are 4, 5, and 6, and so on. The players will be given a certain amount of time to place as few or as many bets as they desire. Players can place bets directly on a number or group of numbers, or they can place bets on certain "propositions" on the outside of the layout. The dealer will then spin the ball. At a certain moment the dealer will announce: "No more bets." At that time, no more bets may be placed. As the ball finishes its spin and descends into the pockets where it ultimately stops in one pocket, the dealer will announce the winning number and its color. He will put a special marker on the winning number. The dealer will collect all the losing bets and then pay off all the winning bets. He will then remove the marker, and the procedure begins all over again.

It is that simple. Roulette has a multitude of bets, most coming in with a high house edge of 5.26 or 2.70 percent (depending on the wheel you play). That's the bad news. The good news is that roulette is a relatively leisurely game with a somewhat slow pace, so the casino doesn't get more than 3050 decisions in an hour.

The Bets of Roulette

The Straight Up Bet: You bet one or more numbers by placing your wager directly on the number or numbers you wish to wager. Winning numbers are paid off at 35 to 1.

Split Bet: Your wager is placed on a line between two numbers. If either number comes up, you are paid at 17 to 1. A split can also be made between 0 and 00 on the American wheel by placing a wager between them.

Three Number Bet: A single bet on any one of three numbers. Place your wager on the outside border of the three numbers on which you wish to bet. Winning numbers are paid off at 11 to 1.

Four Number Bet: This wager can only be made on numbers that form a square. You place your bet at the intersection where all four numbers meet.

The Five Number Bet: This bet only appears on the double-zero layout. It is a single bet that one of the top five numbers (0, 00, 1, 2, or 3) will win on the next spin. You make this bet by placing your chips where the line between the 0 and the 3 meets the border of the layout. The bet pays off at six to one. The casino has a higher edge on this bet of approximately 8 percent.

Six Number Bet: Place this wager on the outside borders of the numbers on the line that separates the two sets of numbers. You are betting that one of those six numbers will hit on the next spin of the ball. This bet pays off at five to one.

The Column Bet: This is a single bet that one of the *columns* of numbers on the layout will contain the number that hits. You place this bet at the bottom of the column in the area that says two to one. This wager pays off at two to one.

The Dozens Bet: Here you are wagering that the winning number will be within a dozen consecutive numbers on the layout. You place this wager in the areas labeled *First Dozen, Second Dozen,* or *Third Dozen.* If any one number in your dozens bet hits, you are paid off at two to one.

The Odd or Even Bets: This bet is placed on the section of the layout labeled *Odd* or *Even.* The bet pays off at even money.

High or Low Bets: Place this wager in the boxes marked either 1–18 or 19–36. It is a wager as to whether the high numbers or the low numbers will contain the winning hit. The bet is paid off at even money.

Red or Black Bets: This bet is placed on the area indicating red or black and is a wager that the winning number will be either a red one or a black one. The bet is paid off at even money.

Surrender or En Prison Options: Some casinos will only take half your losing bet on the outside "even-money" bets of red/black, odd/even, and high/low if the 0 or 00 is the winner. (The difference between surrender and en prison is this: in surrender, the casino immediately takes half your bet; in en prison, the casino locks up your bet for the next spin or until it wins or loses. If it wins, you keep the bet but do not get paid; if it loses, you lose the bet.) This effectively reduces the house edge to 2.63 on the American double-zero wheel and 1.35 on the European single zero wheel.

The Ten-Minutes-or-Less Roulette Strategy

1. If the casino offers surrender or en prison, then only play the outside "proposition" bets of red/black, odd/even, and high/low.
2. If the casino does not offer the above options, then look to reduce the total number of decisions you play by incorporating a "trend" system on the "proposition" bets. A "trend" system can be as follows: if red hits, bet

black on the next spin. If black hits, bet red on the next spin. Then repeat. Trend systems do not have any effect on the house edge but they will reduce the number of decisions you play and thus reduce your overall losing expectation. I suggest you bet with the trend.

3. If you wish to bet directly on the inside numbers, then bet the numbers that have been hitting. You'll find these on the scoreboard at many casinos. There is a rare (I repeat, rare), but valid, possibility that the numbers are hitting because the wheel is a little off or the dealer is somehow influencing what is coming up. Do not bet numbers because you think they are due. They are not.

4. Be aware that when you bet on the inside numbers, the pattern of the game is to lose a lot of decisions and hit a few for big money—but not enough to give you a long-term advantage. On the outside "even-money" proposition bets, the pattern is to win some and lose some, with the losses slowly dominating because of the house edge. The "even-money" bets are *not* 50/50 propositions. You win 18 and lose 20 on the American wheel and you win 18 and lose 19 on the European wheel.

For More Information on Roulette

Spin Roulette Gold: Secrets of the Wheel by Frank Scoblete (Bonus Books, $14.95): The most comprehensive roulette book; explains the game thoroughly. Discusses why most betting systems fail to defeat the game, and then explores how biased wheel and other "advantage-play" techniques can be utilized to get the edge. Has tens of thousands of spins recorded from actual roulette wheels to test your systems against.

Get the Edge at Roulette: How to Predict Were the Ball Will Land! by Christopher Pawlicki (Bonus Books, $13.95): Just what the title says, this book shows you methods that can be used to predict the probability of the ball landing in specific pockets or sectors of the wheel. An advanced book and one every roulette player should own.

Baccarat and Mini-Baccarat

The objective of baccarat is for the players to guess correctly which of three possible propositions will win on the next round: *Bank, Player,* or *Tie.* Two cards are dealt to the *Bank* hand, and two cards are dealt to the *Player* hand. Sometimes a third card is dealt to either or both hands. Whichever hand is closest to nine is the winner. The game is usually dealt from a six- or eight-deck shoe. All 10s, Jacks, Queens, and Kings equal nine. The Ace equals one. All the other cards equal their face value. Thus, a 9 equals nine, a 2 equals two, and so forth.

After the *Bank* and *Player* hands have received two cards, it is possible that either or both might need to draw an extra card. The rules for drawing cards are *predetermined* and essentially irrelevant because the players do not get to make any decisions. Whether or not a card is drawn, at the end of the deal, the hand that totals nine or closest to nine wins.

A winning *Player* hand is paid off at one to one. Thus, if you bet $10, you win $10. A winning *Bank* hand is paid off at 0.95 to 1. This means that if you bet $10, you win $9.50. Another way to look at the *Bank* wager is to consider it a one-to-one payout *minus a 5 percent commission* on winning bets. This commission is collected after the shoe is finished. The *Tie* hand is paid at eight to one. Thus a winning tie bet of $10 will return $80. If you bet on either *Bank* or *Player* and the *Tie* wins, you do not lose your bet. It is a push.

The *Tie* bet has a 14.1 percent edge in favor of the casino. Because intelligent players never make the tie bet, we can judge baccarat based on its two main bets in relation to each other and forget all about the *Tie* bet. The house has a 1.36

percent edge on the *Player* bet and a 1.17 percent edge on the *Bank* bet when the bank charges a 5 percent commission.

The difference between baccarat and mini-baccarat is simple. Baccarat is played on the large table in the high-roller rooms of casinos for table minimums of $25, $50, $100, or more. The game is slow-moving and ritualistic, and the players actually get to deal the cards. Mini-baccarat, on the other hand, is played at a blackjack-style table with the house dealer dealing the cards. It is played for minimums of $5, $10, and $25, but rarely more. Mini-baccarat is an *extremely* fast game!

The Ten-Minutes-or-Less Baccarat Strategy

1. If you can afford it and it is available, always play the traditional game of baccarat in the high-roller room. Because of its slow speed, the small casino edges are manageable.
2. Always bet *Bank*.
3. Try to bet $25 or $75, and ask the casino if you can pay the commission on winning *Bank* bets as you go. Often, casinos will not take the full commission out of $25 and $75 winning *Bank* bets because this entails giving out quarters. (Five percent of $25 is $1.25, so the casino drops the 25 cents and pays you $24 instead of $23.75. Five percent of $75 is $3.75, so the casino drops the 75 cents and pays you $72.) By not paying the full commission on winning *Bank* bets, you get to reduce the casino edge to almost 0.5 percent on the *Bank*.
4. If you must play mini-baccarat, try to reduce the number of decisions by sitting out at least half of the rounds. You can do this by playing a "trending" system where you'll only bet *Bank* after a *Bank* win or after two *Player* losses, etc. As with any "trend" system, the house edge is not affected, but the total number of deci-

sions is reduced, thereby reducing your exposure to the house edge over time.

5. Never bet *Tie*.

For More Information on Baccarat and Mini-Baccarat

Baccarat Battle Book by Frank Scoblete (Bonus Books, $12.95): Comprehensive analysis of baccarat and mini-baccarat that discusses how to get a "monetary edge" by utilizing *Bank* bets in conjunction with comps. Has a complete analysis of card counting systems that have been developed for baccarat as well as interviews with Henry Tamburin, author of the recommended *Winning Baccarat Strategies* (Research Services Unlimited, $19.95), and John May, author of the recommended *Baccarat for the Clueless* (Carol Publishing, $12.00), concerning their research into possible methods of beating the game.

Keno

Many casino games can be traced to antiquity; still others are associated with specific historical moments in time and place. Today's casino game of Keno is one such game, with its roots in Chinese prehistory and history, as well as a specific historical significance for Americans. In China, a game very similar to Keno has been played for several thousand years—by emperors, warlords, merchants, and peasants. Even communists have been known to try to make some capital from picking "the numbers" although such activities are frowned upon by the party bosses (known in Chinese as party poopers). The name of the Chinese game was and is Kino.

In the 1800s, when the American West was being conquered by, and then connected to, civilization, and the railroads were being built, cheap labor was imported from China, and with it was also imported the game of Kino. It was so popular with the Chinese laborers that soon enterprising Americans, seeing the incredible profits that could accrue from winning said laborers' hard-earned pay, took over the game, changed its name to Keno, and set up "Keno parlors" throughout the West. Keno was known as the "Chinese Lottery," and, like any lottery, it was a boon to its owners and a bane to its players. At one time, just about every town in the West had a Keno parlor.

Still, for those of you who enjoy playing lotteries, or local charity chance books, or if numbers are your thing, the casino game of Keno might hold some interest for you. It is indeed the equivalent of a lottery, but much faster! You do not have to wait a few days for the results, just a few minutes. Of course, like the lottery, Keno comes in with very high edges for the house—around 25 percent, more or less, depending on the casino where the game is being played and the type of wagers being pursued.

The players' tickets are numbered 1 through 80. You can choose to play between 1 and 20 numbers on a given ticket. The numbers to be played are "Xed" out in crayon (back to childhood we go!). To win a multi-number bet, you often do not have to select all the numbers, just some of them. Here are some of the most popular betting options at Keno:

Types of Bets at Keno

Straight Ticket: A player can mark one or more numbers on a ticket.

Split Ticket: A player can bet on two or more groups of numbers on a single ticket by circling the groups to be played.

Way Ticket: Combining several groups of numbers on the same ticket.

Combination Ticket: The player selects two or more groups of numbers and indicates how the groups are to be combined to form many tickets within one ticket.

King Ticket: The player selects one number to be used with all the other groups that have been indicated.

Multi-Race Ticket: This is a ticket that indicates that it will be played for two or more sessions in a row.

Sometimes I receive mailings from individuals who are selling systems to beat Keno. They claim that they have found patterns to the numbers that can be exploited by their "super-seven Keno buster" or their "Keno pyramid" method or their "ping-pong power play." The costs of these systems are—to say the least—exorbitant. The claims of the systems are—to be frank—bogus. Is there a magical system for beating Keno? Sorry, no. The system sellers are scamming us. The Keno numbers are selected randomly, either by air-driven ping-pong balls (just like many state lotteries) or by computer. The fact that some numbers may have hit several times and other numbers may not have shown their faces for quite a while is no indication that a number will continue to hit or is due to hit. Picking numbers is sheer guesswork.

Why play Keno? First, it offers a relaxing atmosphere. Keno lounges are usually pleasantly appointed places, with comfortable chairs. You can drink a cup of coffee, pick your numbers in a leisurely fashion, and not worry about other players telling you what to do or what not to do. Played properly for small stakes, Keno, even with its abominably high house edges, will not drain your gambling bankroll any time soon, as it is the snail of casino games.

And, like anything in life, there are better ways to approach a Keno game. Walter Thomason, in his excellent book *109 Ways to Beat the Casinos* (Bonus Books, $13.95), gives some great advice when it comes to Keno. "Do not select more than eight numbers on a straight ticket. The odds of hitting all eight are 230,000 to 1—but the odds of hitting all nine out of nine numbers are 1.3 million to 1! Bet way tickets rather than straight tickets. The odds are the same, but you'll hit more payoffs."

The Ten-Minutes-or-Less Keno Strategy

1. Play the minimum amount allowed, which is usually a dollar or two, as the house edge is very big at Keno—25 percent, more or less. Luckily, the game is slow, maybe one game per 6 to 10 minutes.
2. If you are betting on several numbers, always have them in some kind of small or large sequence, as you'll note how often numbers run in sequence (but the game is still random!). This can be done on "way" tickets as well. "Sequencing" does not improve the odds, as non-sequences are just as likely to occur, but when you "sequence," the thrill as a number hits is greater (at least my mother finds that to be so!).
3. Use Keno as a break from more adrenaline-producing games, when you want to stay in the action but you need a little rest from betting serious money.
4. Video Keno, while much faster than regular Keno, has much better paybacks—more like your typical slot machine. However, you can play video Keno so fast that the speed makes up for the decrease in the house edge. My advice is to stick with the slow game and relax, have a cup of coffee, or read a paper between games.
5. Avoid betting the multi-race ticket. Do not get caught up in Keno mania, the desire to hit your "lucky" numbers. Some people obsess that if they play the same numbers over and over, sooner or later these numbers will hit. They then fear *not to play* lest their numbers hit when they aren't on them. To forestall Keno mania, do not play the same combination of numbers all the time.

Mix them up and try—do try—*not* to remember which numbers you played in previous games. Bet one game at a time only!

For More Information About Keno

Guerrilla Gambling: How to Beat the Casinos at Their Own Games by Frank Scoblete (Bonus Books, $12.95): A small chapter of this book discusses the various tickets in some depth.

109 Ways to Beat the Casinos edited by Walter Thomason (Bonus Books, $13.95): This book contains short, specific tips by some of gambling's best writers, including Henry Tamburin, Fred Renzey, John Grochowski, Frank Scoblete, Alene Paone, and Walter Thomason.

Three-Card Poker

Several new games seem to have caught on with enough people that they are hanging around, and some are even becoming player favorites. One such is Three-Card Poker, a game that offers the player table-game action without any annoying or complex strategy decisions associated with real poker. Indeed, the Three-Card Poker player places his bets and hopes, basically. Thus, he is much like a slot player or a baccarat player. The objective of Three-Card Poker is to beat the dealer's three-card hand. There is also an added incentive in attempting to win bonuses for certain premium hands.

The game is quite simple to understand. The player can bet on three propositions called *Ante, Play,* and the independent *Pair Plus.* The dealer deals the player three cards and himself three cards. If a player has opted to place an *Ante* bet, when he looks at his three cards he must decide whether to stay in the game or fold. To stay, he must place a bet equal to his *Ante* bet in the *Play* square. That means, appropriately, that the player is playing. Now the dealer turns over his three cards. If the player beats the dealer's three-card hand, the player wins the *Ante* bet at even money (i.e., you win one dollar for every one dollar wagered). The *Play* pays a bonus for certain premium hands, such as a Straight Flush (usually 40 to 1), Three of a Kind (usually 30 to 1), a Straight (usually 6 to 1), and a Flush (usually 4 to 1). The *Play* also pays even money for a Pair.

The *Pair Plus* bet is a side bet that can be made without placing an *Ante* bet. If the player has a *Pair Plus*, which is two of a kind or better, he receives an additional payout. Many of these payouts are greater than one to one. For example, Three of a Kind pays four to one, and a Straight Flush pays five to one.

While most Three-Card Poker payouts are relatively standard in casinos throughout the country, there are some differences here and there. Check the table layout before you play to see what the hands are returning. One caveat that is quite favorable to the player in the game concerns dealer qualification. Unlike Caribbean Stud (see next chapter), in which a dealer not qualifying for play cancels winning player hands, in Three-Card Poker, a nonqualifying dealer is a boon to the players. What qualifies a dealer? Simply, if the dealer does not have at least a Queen high or better hand, the players win on all their bets. The house edge on the *Ante* and *Play* part of the game is around 2 percent. However, this can be a very fast game, and 90 decisions in an hour is not that rare.

The Ten-Minutes-or-Less Three-Card Poker Strategy

1. Always bet *Play* when you have a Queen or better.
2. Avoid the *Pair Plus* bet, as it merely increases the amount you're wagering but does not add to your

expectation. In fact, it just adds more money to the casino coffers as the game is quite fast and the edge on Pair Plus is 2.3 percent.

For More Information on Three-Card Poker

Bold Card Play: Best Strategies for Caribbean Stud, Let It Ride and Three Card Poker by Frank Scoblete (Bonus Books, $12.95): This book has the complete analysis of Three-Card Poker based on the inventor's specs and explains the effects of different strategy choices on the house edge.

Casino War

Hard as it is to believe, that kid game you might have played has made its way into the casinos. I'm wondering when those "crazy games" that Chevy Chase played in *National Lampoon's Las Vegas Vacation* will begin showing up. (What *is* the basic strategy for Rock, Scissors, and Paper anyway?) Because I have seen Casino War now at over a half dozen places, I guess it deserves its own space in a book.

The game is usually played with six decks, although sometimes you might find fewer decks. The fewer the decks, the better for the player using my strategy. All cards have their regular ranking with the Ace high, deuce low. The dealer deals the player and himself a card. Whichever card is higher, wins. No-brainer for this part of the game.

Strategy comes in if there is a tie. The player has the option to give up half his bet or "go to war." If the player goes to war, he must match his initial bet. The dealer will now give the player and himself another card. If the player wins the "war," or even ties the dealer on this second round, his second bet is paid off at even money, but his first bet is returned to him (it is considered a push). If the dealer beats the player, then the player loses both his initial bet and his second bet. You also have the option of betting a tie, but, like baccarat, the tie is a very bad bet with a house edge that is about 19 percent.

The Ten-Minutes-or-Less Casino War Strategy

1. Go to war on all the ties. Never give up half your initial wager.
2. Because this game can be played at lightning speed, you have to try to take your time putting the money on the layout—and when there's a tie, take your time "deciding" whether to go to war.

Chapter 5

The Moderate Games

Caribbean Stud

Caribbean Stud is offered on a blackjack-like table, and all players play against the house. The objective of the game is to beat the dealer's hand by making the best possible poker hand with five cards. There are two betting squares in front of each player—one labeled "ante" and one labeled "bet." There is also a side bet, the "jackpot," which is made by dropping a one dollar chip in the jackpot slot. This bet is for a progressive jackpot that increases with each hand played. The jackpot side bet is strictly optional.

The game begins with the players putting a bet in the ante square and, if they wish, a dollar in the jackpot bet. The dealer deals five cards to each player, face down. The dealer also deals himself five cards, the last card dealt face up. The players check their cards. They now have a choice:

1. They can play out their hands.
2. They can surrender their hands and lose their *antes.*

If they decide to play out their hands, they must place a bet that is *double* their ante in the "bet" square. After the players have made their respective decisions, the dealer turns over his remaining four cards and makes the best poker hand possible out of them. The one caveat is that the dealer must have at least an Ace-King hand for the game to be decided fully—this is called the dealer-qualifying rule. If he fails to have such a hand, he pays off the antes and pushes on the bets. If the dealer achieves a hand of Ace-King (or better), then all the players' hands are judged against it. If the player cannot beat the dealer's hand, the player loses both his ante and his bet. If the player beats the dealer, the ante is paid off at even money, while the bet is paid off at house odds—these odds will be listed at the table.

In addition, if the player originally opted for the jackpot side bet, certain select hands will win a bonus award, up to and including the jackpot itself.

Utilizing my strategy that follows, the casino will have an approximate 2.7 percent edge over the player. Although the game is relatively leisurely, that dealer-qualifying rule can sometimes be very frustrating when you have a premium hand, only to discover that the dealer has not qualified and you just win the ante.

The Ten-Minutes-or-Less Caribbean Stud Strategy

1. Surrender any hand that is lower than an Ace-King.
2. Bet any Ace-King or better.
3. Never make the jackpot side bet.

For More Information on Caribbean Stud

Bold Card Play: Best Strategies for Caribbean Stud, Let It Ride and Three Card Poker by Frank Scoblete (Bonus Books, $12.95): This book has the complete analysis of Caribbean Stud Poker and explains the effects of different strategy choices on the house edge. Also has a more complete basic strategy for the game and explains when the jackpot bet will go "positive."

Let It Ride

The objective of Let It Ride is to make the best poker hand that is a pair of 10s or better with your three cards and the two community cards. You are not playing to beat the dealer, merely to get a good hand that pays a bonus according to a set payoff schedule. This bonus schedule applies to all hands. If, at the end of play, you have three bets working, you will receive the bonus on all three bets. If you only have one bet working, you will only receive the bonus on that one bet.

To play Let It Ride, you'll need three times the amount of the table minimum because each round requires three initial bets. However, as play progresses, you will have the option of removing two of the three bets. In front of each player are three betting squares labeled "1," "2," and "$." After the players have placed their bets, the dealer deals each player three cards and puts two cards face down as "community" cards. The players now look at their three-card hands.

They can now decide to withdraw their number "1" bet or let it ride. Once the players have decided, the dealer turns over the first of the two community cards. Again the players can now decide whether to take off their number "2" bet or let it ride. Finally, the dealer turns over the second community card and the players are paid off according to the posted payoff schedule. The "$" bet cannot be called off—it is the bet that gives the casino its edge, thus making it live up to its symbol.

Most casinos offer a jackpot for an additional side bet of $1, as is done with Caribbean Stud. You place this bet at the beginning of the round, and it is not returnable as are bets number "1" and number "2." It is paid based on a separate formula for premium hands. The layout for Let It Ride will contain all the payout information for the regular game and the jackpot option. With my basic strategy, the player will face a house edge that is approximately 3 percent. The game is also relatively fast, so that 3 percent will be working on between 60 and 90 decisions per hour. Another thing to note is that Let It Ride will see the player win approximately one quarter of his hands. In other words, three of every four hands will be losers. The hands the player wins, however, will often be for tidy sums, especially if he has been able to "let it ride" from the first bet.

The Ten-Minutes-or-Less
Let It Ride Strategy

1. On bet #1, let it ride if you have the following cards:
   a. Pair of 10s or better
   b. Any three cards to a Royal Flush
   c. Any three cards in succession to a Straight Flush

2. On bet #2, let it ride if you have the following:
   a. Pair of 10s or better
   b. Any four cards to a Royal Flush
   c. Any four cards to a Straight Flush
   d. Any four cards to a Flush

3. One caveat is to note that some casinos limit the total amount of money they will pay out for a Royal Flush and other premium hands. Make sure that when you are betting you do not bet more money than the casino will pay out should you win. If, for example, the limit were $25,000, you would not want to bet $30 per hand, as a winning Royal Flush pays one thousand to one. In this case, if you win, it *should* be $30,000, but because of the "cap" the casino will not pay you more than $25,000.

4. Do not bet the jackpot side bet.

For More Information on Let It Ride

Bold Card Play: Best Strategies for Caribbean Stud, Let It Ride and Three Card Poker by Frank Scoblete (Bonus Books, $12.95): This book has the complete analysis of Let It Ride and explains the effects of different strategy choices on the house edge. Also has a more complete basic strategy for the game.

Pai Gow Poker

Pai Gow Poker is the card version of a very popular Asian game known as Pai Gow (tricky, tricky renaming). The game is played with a 52-card deck and one Joker. The Joker can only be used as an Ace or to complete a Straight, a Flush, or a Straight Flush. Each player must make two poker hands that rank higher than the dealer's two poker hands. Each player receives seven cards that must be split into a *High* hand consisting of five cards, and a *Low* hand consisting of two cards. The ranking of hands follows the traditional poker rankings for the *High* hand. Thus, a Royal Straight Flush is the highest hand. For the *Low* hand, the highest-ranking hand is two Aces.

A player may opt to be the *Bank,* in which case that player must pay the other players on winning hands and collect the losing hands for himself. The casino will assess a 5 percent tax on all winnings. If no player is the *Bank,* the casino will bank all the bets. No player can be the *Bank* for every hand.

Before the deal of the cards, three dice are shaken, and the results determine the order of the deal. Each player is then dealt seven cards from which to make two hands as indicated above. The rank of the *High* hand must be higher than the rank of the *Low* hand. The casino dealer must set her hand according to a fixed set of rules. Even if a player is banking the table, the casino dealer still plays. If no player is banking the table, the casino will bank it. Also, the bank (be it the dealer or a player) wins all *copies* (ties)—where both the *High* hand and *Low* hand are identical.

Because you have to win both hands to win, it is important to realize that a powerhouse draw must be split into two strong hands. For example, if you are given four Aces and the Joker, that means that you now have five Aces—an unbeatable five-card hand. However, what good does it do to win the *High* hand only to lose the *Low* hand? No good. Thus, the intelligent choice is to split the five Aces, putting three in the *High* hand (a strong hand) and two in the *Low* hand (an unbeatable hand).

Although not set in stone, the house usually has a 2.5 percent edge over the average Pai Gow Poker player. The good news is that the game is *very* slow, with many no-decision hands.

The Ten-Minutes-or-Less Pai Gow Poker Strategy

1. Always break up "powerhouse" hands into two *strong* hands. Remember that you must win both hands to win.
2. Keep in mind that the five-card hand *High* must be stronger than the two-card *Low* hand. Thus, you cannot have two Kings in the *Low* hand and an Ace high in the *High* hand.
3. When in doubt, ask the dealer to set your hands according to "house rules." This is the easiest way to learn how to play your hands.

For Further Information About Pai Gow Poker

Guerrilla Gambling: How to Beat the Casinos at Their Own Games by Frank Scoblete (Bonus Books, $12.95): Goes into detail about setting the hands and operating as the bank.

Craps

The most exciting, yet most intimidating, game in the casino, craps, is witnessing a surge of popularity due to the belief that some shooters can change the odds of the game to favor the players by reason of their "rhythmic rolling" or "precision shooting" (I believe! I believe!). Be that as it may, the majority of craps players play the game so poorly that no amount of "dice control" can overcome the huge house edges that they are giving the casinos. And that doesn't have to be the case, because at its purest craps is a very simple game with a very small house edge on its better bets.

Despite its appearance, craps is as easy as 1-2-3. The *Pass Line* that goes around the whole table and the *Don't Pass Line* that mirrors it are the two basic bets of craps.

The game starts with the shooter placing one or the other of these bets. Because most players are "right bettors" (they bet the *Pass Line*), let us look at the game from the perspective of the *Pass Line*. The player is given the dice. The shooter now rolls the dice. If he rolls a 7 or an 11, the *Pass Line* bettors win even money—i.e., if you bet $10, you win $10. The *Don't Pass* bettors lose. However, if the shooter rolls a 2, 3, or 12, the *Pass Line* bettors lose and, on the 2 or 3, the *Don't Pass* bettors win; on the 12, the *Don't Pass* bettors push, neither winning nor losing.

If the shooter rolls any one of the following numbers: 4, 5, 6, 8, 9, or 10, this number becomes the *point*. For the *Pass Line* bettor to win, the shooter must roll that number again before he rolls a 7. The reverse holds true for the *Don't Pass* bettor. If a 7 is rolled before the point, the *Don't Pass* bettor wins.

If the shooter "sevens out," the dice are passed on to the next shooter. If the shooter hits his point, he "comes out" again, just as in the above.

That is the game, pure and simple.

Playing the *Pass* or *Don't Pass* gives the casino an approximate 1.4 percent edge. However, the player can reduce the edge even more by taking advantage of the "Free Odds" bet option. Here is an example of how this option works.

The 7 can be made six different ways with two dice. The 5 can be made four different ways. Thus, the odds of a 7 appearing in relation to a 5 are six ways to four ways, or three to two. Once the shooter has established his point number (let us keep it as the 5), the player has the option of placing an amount equal to (single odds), twice as much (double or 2X odds), three times as much (triple or 3X odds), five times as much (5X odds), 10 times as much (10X odds), 20 times as much (20X odds), or 100 times (100X odds) or more, as his *Pass Line* bet in "odds" immediately behind it. The casino determines how much "odds" it will allow. Let's analyze the bet based on double odds.

The point is 5 and you have $10 on the *Pass Line*. You can now place $20 in odds behind it. If the shooter rolls a 5, you will be paid even money for your $10 *Pass Line* bet and the true odds for the Odds bet—thus, you would win $30 for your $20 Odds bet. The casino has no edge on this bet. The Free Odds bet reduces the casino edge on the *Pass Line* as follows:

BET	CASINO EDGE
Pass Line with no odds	1.41%
Pass Line with 1X odds	0.85%
Pass Line with 2X odds	0.61%
Pass Line with 3X odds	0.47%
Pass Line with 5X odds	0.33%
Pass Line with 10X odd	0.18%
Pass Line with 20X odds	0.10%
Pass Line with 100X odds	0.02%

The true odds for the point numbers are as follows:

Number	Ways to Make	Ways to Make Seven	Odds
4	3	6	2 to 1
5	4	6	3 to 2
6	5	6	6 to 5
8	5	6	6 to 5
9	4	6	3 to 2
10	3	6	2 to 1

Two other low-percentage bets are the *Come* and *Don't Come* bets. These bets function in exactly the same way and have exactly the same house edges as the *Pass* and *Don't Pass* bets. The only difference is that they are made *after* the point is established. Once the shooter has a point, you can place a bet in the large *Come* area on the layout or on the smaller *Don't Come* area in the upper left- and right-hand corners of the layout. A 7 or 11 wins the *Come* bet at even money and loses the *Don't Come* bet. A 2, 3, or 12 loses the *Come* bet, while the 2 or 3 wins the *Don't Come* bet. Again, 12 is a push. However, should one of the point numbers be rolled (i.e., 4, 5, 6, 8, 9, or 10), that number now must be rolled before the 7 for the *Come* bettor to win. Should the 7 appear before the number, the *Don't Come* bettor wins. The *Come–Don't Come* is merely a game within a game. As with the *Pass* and *Don't Pass*, the *Come* and *Don't Come* players are also offered the option of Free Odds.

The last of the low-percentage bets is the *placing* of the 6 and/or 8, which can be done at any time. Here you simply place a wager in multiples of $6. The casino will pay off a winning bet at "casino odds" of $7 for every $6 wagered. The casino edge on this bet is 1.52 percent. You can place a number at any time, and you can also call the bet off or take it down at any time.

Types of Bets at Craps

The following bets can be placed at any time, including during the come-out roll. The edges on most of these are prohibitive.

Place the 4: You place the 4 in multiples of five dollars. If the 4 is rolled before the 7, the player wins nine dollars. The house edge is 6.67 percent. Too much.

Place the 5: You place the 5 in multiples of five dollars. If the 5 rolls before a 7, the player wins seven dollars. Casino edge is 4 percent. Too much.

Place the 6: As stated, you place the 6 in multiples of six dollars. If the 6 rolls before a 7, the player wins seven dollars. Casino edge is 1.52 percent. Okay.

Place the 8: As stated, you place the 8 in multiples of six dollars. If the 8 rolls before a 7, the player wins seven dollars. Casino edge is 1.52 percent. Okay.

Place the 9: You place the 9 in multiples of five dollars. If the 9 rolls before a 7, the player wins seven dollars. Casino edge is 4 percent. Too much.

Place the 10: You place the 10 in multiples of five dollars. If the 10 is rolled before the 7, the player wins nine dollars. The house edge is 6.67 percent. Too much.

Place to Lose

You also can place the numbers to lose. Sometimes this is called *laying* the numbers, as in: "Lay the 4!" In such a case, you are rooting for a 7 to be thrown before the number appears.

Place the 4 to Lose: Here you bet in multiples of $11 that the 7 will come up before the 4. If you win, you receive five dollars. The house edge is 3.03 percent. Too much.

Place the 5 to Lose: Here you bet in multiples of eight dollars that the 7 will come up before the 5. If you win, you the bet is paid off at five dollars. The house edge is 2.5 percent. Marginal.

Place the 6 to Lose: Here you are betting in multiples of five dollars that the 7 will be rolled before the 6. If you win, the bet is paid off at four dollars. The house edge is 1.82 percent. Okay.

Place the 8 to Lose: Here you are betting in multiples of five dollars that the 7 will be rolled before the 8. If you win, the bet is paid off at four dollars. The house edge is 1.82 percent. Okay.

Place the 9 to Lose: Here you bet in multiples of eight dollars that the 7 will come up before the 9. If you win, the bet is paid off at five dollars. The house edge is 2.5 percent. Marginal.

Place the 10 to Lose: Here you bet in multiples of $11 that the 7 will come up before the 10. If you win, you receive five dollars. The house edge is 3.03 percent. Too much.

Proposition Bets

Hard 4: You are betting that the 4 will be made as 2:2 before a 7 is rolled or before the 4 is rolled as 3:1 or 1:3. Pays 7 to 1. House edge is 11.11 percent. Awful.

Hard 6: You are betting that the 6 will be made as 3:3 before a 7 is rolled or before the 6 is made as 5:1, 1:5, 4:2, or 2:4. Pays 9 to 1. House edge is 9.09 percent. Awful.

Hard 8: You are betting that the 8 will be made as 4:4 before the 7 is rolled or before the 8 is rolled as 5:3, 3:5, 6:2, or 2:6. Pays 9 to 1. House edge is 9.09 percent. Awful.

Hard 10: You are betting that the 10 will be made as 5:5 before a 7 is rolled or before the 10 is rolled as 6:4 or 4:6. Pays 7 to 1. House edge is 11.11 percent. Awful.

One-Roll Proposition Bets

The bets listed are one-roll wagers and the usual payoff for them. Some casinos will pay at a higher rate. The more the casino pays, the lower the house edge.

The Field: A one-roll wager that the next number will be one of the Field numbers: 2, 3, 4, 9, 10, 11, or 12. Sometimes the 5 is substituted for the 9. If the 2 or 12 hits, the bet is paid off at 2 to 1. The other numbers are paid off at 1 to 1. The house edge is 5.26 percent. Too much.

The 2: A one-roll wager that the next number will be a 2. Pays off at 30 to 1. The house edge is 13.89 percent. Truly awful.

Hard 4 Hop: A one-roll wager that the next number will be a 4 made as 2:2. Pays off at 30 to 1. The house edge is 13.89 percent. Truly awful.

Hard 6 Hop: A one-roll wager that the next number will be a 6 made as 3:3. Pays off at 30 to 1. The house edge is 13.89 percent. Truly awful.

Hard 8 Hop: A one-roll wager that the next number will be an 8 made as 4:4. Pays off at 30 to 1. The house edge is 13.89 percent. Truly awful.

Hard 10 Hop: A one-roll wager that the next number will be a 10 made as 5:5. Pays off at 30 to 1. The house edge is 13.89 percent.

The 12: A one-roll wager that the next number will be a 12. Pays off at 30 to 1. The house edge is 13.89 percent. Truly awful.

The 3: A one-roll wager that the next number will be a 3. Pays off at 15 to 1. The house edge is 11.11 percent. Awful.

The 11: A one-roll wager that the next number will be an 11. Pays off at 15 to 1. The house edge is 11.11 percent. Awful.

Any Craps: A one-roll wager that the next number will be a craps: 2, 3, or 12. Pays off at 7 to 1. The house edge is 11.11 percent. Awful.

Any 7: A one-roll wager that the next number will be a 7. Pays off at 4 to 1. House edge is 16.67 percent. Wins the prize as the worst bet at craps!

Horn Bet: A one-roll wager that the next number will be a 2, 3, 11, or 12. House pays off at the odds for the individual number as shown earlier. House edge is a combined 12.50 percent. Awful.

The Language of Craps

Most people in America speak English. Many speak Spanish. Still others speak French or German or Italian or Hindi or Mandarin or Japanese or any one of over a hundred languages and dialects that can be found in the home of the brave and the land of the free. Of course, everyone is proud of his or her language, as language and culture go hand in hand. Who thinks his or her culture is *not* the greatest thing in the world? ("I'm proud to be a Gugnodo! We built the first mounds of dung before the pyramids appeared!")

Poor fools. Poor deluded fools.

Don't they know that while their languages are okay (after all, in most of them you can call a taxi, order some food, tell the spouse to take out the garbage, and invade that village over there), there is only one language that has the color, charm, fantasy, enthusiasm, and descriptive power to make it the number one language in the world, or at least that part of the world worth discussing. Of course, I mean the casino world. And its greatest language is known as "the lingo of craps."

As with all great languages, craps has its own dictionary (you know a language has made it when it has a whole book devoted to it!), a slim volume titled *A Guide to Craps Lingo: From Snake Eyes to Muleteeth.* What Webster did for the English language, Chris Fagans and David Guzman did for craps.

Once you have read this book, you will be truly bilingual. You'll be able to speak your inferior language and the superior language of craps.

Let me give you some linguistic enlightenment:

Of course, everyone knows what "snakes eyes" means (your daughter's boyfriend), and everyone has heard of "yo" as in Rocky's classic comment after he suffered serious brain damage: "Yo, Adrian, I did it!" Poor Rocky, when asked what he actually had done, couldn't quite remember. So he said, "yo-eleven" which he thought was the round in which he had been knocked out. And that's how "yo-eleven" became a craps call. In honor of really stupid New Yorkers, the 11 is sometimes referred to as a Jedi Master, "Yo-Duh."

And did you know that "Little Joe" is not just a character on the old *Bonanza* series but another way to say "four." You could also say "Tutu." No, not in honor of the South African bishop or to describe what a ballet dancer wears, but, again, as another way to say "four."

Remember that old Rosemary Clooney song, "You Give Me Fever"? Well, I was five when I first heard it and, guess what—that's what fever means in craps—a "five." So when you put your bet down for a "five," just say: "I got a fever for you." Of course, if the dealer doesn't know what that means, he might think you're coming on to him or he might get upset because he thinks you have some rare tropical disease, or both. Here's a colorfully disgusting call from a stickman when the "five" rolls: "Five! It'*snot* in the field, clean it up!"

The number "six" doesn't have many really good synonyms but "the lumber number" certainly conjures images in the imagination best left unwritten.

The "seven" is the most dreaded number in craps after the shooter has established which point he is shooting for. It is called the "Devil" and "Big Red." When a shooter rolls the "seven" it can take a player to hell ("do" bettors) or to heaven ("don't" bettors). All craps players know, or should know, that if you say the word "seven" out loud at the table, bad luck will happen—usually in the form of a big, superstitious guy with a wicked left hook aimed at the mouth that is just finishing up saying "seve . . ."—thump!

The "eight" has several colorful appellations. Try these the next time you place the "eight." "Give me a square pair!" "I want two windows." "Make that block fours." When the shooter's number is "eight" and he makes it, dealers can say: "He eight it!" Or, to be more genteel, a dealer might say: "Meet Ada from Decatur."

Speaking of women, when the "nine" is your point and you make it, the dealer can shout: "Nina from Pasadena!" as Nina, plain and without the attendant city, also means "nine." For some reason, a "nine" can be referred to as a "Jesse James," perhaps because he was shot with a .45 (numbers that, when added together, equal nine). And for scurrilous stickmen, the call of "nine" goes: "9-9-9 just like mine!" (Deluded braggart!)

Evidently the British have gotten involved when it comes to the "10," which is labeled variously "Big Ben," "The Ripper," "The Queen's Crown," and something too gross to mention in mixed company or even alone. It is also called "Sunflowers," "Double Nickels," "Venus and Mars," and a "Tennessee Tottie."

Finally, you have the famous "Box Cars," or 12, which can also be called: "Midnight," "The Apostles," "Six-Packs," and "Muleteeth."

Most cultures have a religious component, and some scholars would say that religion and culture go together like a horse and carriage (or was that love and marriage?). Anyway, you will find many religious and moral sayings in the culture of craps, as in this plea to the craps deities: "Come on, baby needs a new pair of shoes!" Of course, baby needs a new pair of shoes because pop is busy playing craps with the shoe money!

"Peace on Earth, good will to men." If you like that saying, the craps equivalent is much easier to understand: "Dice—be nice!" And here is the most dreaded of all craps calls: "The devil jumped up!" That means the nasty 7 just ended a shooters roll.

Craps, like any culture, has many rules to follow. Here are some, which I have dubbed the Ten Commandments of Craps:

1. Never put down a bet when the dice are in the air. If the dice hit the money or the chips, the 7 will result and that big guy I mentioned earlier will be aiming for you.

2. Never talk to a shooter who is about to roll. If you do, that 7 will come up.

3. Never push your way into a game next to a person who is shooting. If you bump him, you know what will happen and you know what big guy will be after you.

4. Never say the word "seven" at a craps table. If you do, it will appear.

5. Never think the word "seven" at a craps table. If you do, it will appear.

6. Never take new dice if a die goes off the table. Ask for "same dice" or guess what will appear?

7. Never dangle your hands over the table because if the dice hit them, the devil will jump up and so will that devilish big guy who punches people.

8. Never delay the game because a hot shooter always cools off during delays and you know what number will come up then. If you cannot figure out what bets you made, do not make them anymore—and take your ginkgo biloba.

9. Never yell at someone who sevens out early. If you do, when it is your turn, you will seven out early too.

10. Never tell people how much money you've won playing craps because they actually will expect you to buy baby a new pair of shoes!

The Ten-Minutes-or-Less Craps Strategy

1. Bet Pass Line for the minimum and back it with as much in odds as you can afford when the point is established. If you plan to bet $15, you are better off betting it as $5 on the Pass Line and $10 in odds, than betting all $15 on the Pass Line.

2. When the point is established, if it is the 6 or the 8, then bet the other in multiples of $6. Say the point is 8. You have $5 plus $10 in odds ($15 total); then bet $12 on the 6. Since the 6 and 8 are the numbers with the second

highest frequency of appearing, you have the best chance of winning on them.

3. When the point is established, if neither is a 6 or 8, then also Place the 6 *and* 8 in multiples of $6. You'll have three numbers working for you, the Pass Line, and the 6 and 8. It will be easy to keep track of your bets this way.

4. If you only want to bet two numbers, simply Place the 6 and 8 in multiples of $6.

5. You should have 10 times the amount of your "spread" as a session stake. Thus, if you are betting $6 on the 6 and 8, you have a "spread" of $12. You should have at least $120 to play with.

6. Ignore all the other bets at the table.

For More Information About Craps

There is a craps revolution going on in America, due in part to savvy craps players' acceptance of the Captain's contentions that some shooters have the ability to change the nature of the odds they face due to their controlled shooting or "rhythmic rolling." I've written about the Captain and his theories in several books and tapes. In addition, the phenomenal analyses and teaching skill of Sharpshooter, a young engineer, and Dominator, Mr. Finesse, and Bill Burton, dice-control experts and teachers who have refined and expanded on the theory and practice of the Captain's methods, have gone a long way toward making craps a beatable game for those in the know. Here, then, is a list of books, tapes, and teaching seminars that I highly recommend. Craps is a good game, even if you do not practice a controlled rhythmic roll; but it is a *great* game when you do!

Beat the Craps Out of the Casinos: How to Play Craps and Win! by Frank Scoblete (Bonus Books, $9.95): The classic, bestselling craps book of all time. Introduces the Captain and discusses his revolutionary methods of play, including the

5-*Count,* the *Supersystem,* and *Pushing the House.* You'll also read about the Captain's Crew of high rollers and the remarkable lady known as "the Arm"—the precision shooter who became a legend in Atlantic City craps circles.

The Captain's Craps Revolution! by Frank Scoblete (Paone Press, $21.95): The follow-up to *Beat the Craps Out of the Casinos,* this is a no-nonsense look at the classic and radical *Supersystems,* a detailed analysis of the 5-*Count* and why it works, an exploration of new bets such as the "Oddsman's bet" and "buying" player don't bets. Has the best Darkside strategy recommended by the Captain for those who play the "don't" side of the game.

Forever Craps: The Five-Step Advantage-Play Method by Frank Scoblete (Bonus Books, $13.95): Five steps that will allow you to achieve a monetary edge over the casinos. This book shows you how to utilize a rhythmic roll or precision shot to flip the house edge in your favor. In addition, it explains how to utilize the 5-*Count* with the Golden Shooter rule to determine which other shooters might be changing the odds—the shooters on whom it is worth risking your money. Full explanation on how to get more comps for less risk. Contains the complete biography of the Captain!

Get the Edge at Craps: How to Control the Dice! by "Sharpshooter" (Bonus Books, $14.95): The definitive book on rhythmic rolling or precision shooting. Sharpshooter shares his research and analysis in an easy-to-assimilate way that will help you learn the most important skill of all—how to make the dice obey your will! Once you've learned the elements of a precision throw—the proper dice sets, the proper grip, the proper launch angle and throw—Sharpshooter shows you how to bet your advantage.

Sharpshooter Craps! by Frank Scoblete (Paone Press, Audio Cassette, 60 minutes, $16.95): This tape discusses how to use the 5-*Count,* how to select a table, how to become a rhythmic roller, how to manage your money, and how to get the mental edge as well.

The Craps Answer Book by John Grochowski (Bonus Books, $13.95): An excellent introduction to the game of craps in an easy-to-assimilate question-and-answer format. Grochowski is a terrific writer, and he sprinkles his lessons with some very interesting information about the origins and practice of craps.

Tina Trapp's Guide to Craps by Larry Edell (Leaf Press, $14.95): You can learn the game of craps and enjoy some of tempestuous Tina's adventures as well. This is a "novel" approach to teaching the game of craps.

Golden Touch Dice Control Seminar: Hands-on instruction in controlled shooting and proper betting by Frank Scoblete, Sharpshooter, Dominator, Bill Burton, Mr. Finesse, Billy the Kid, and more. Call 1-800-944-0406 or 1-866-SET-DICE for a free brochure. You can also find more information at *www.goldentouchcraps.com.*

Chapter 6

The Complex Games

The two games in this chapter are the most complex of those offered by the casinos. More books have been written about blackjack, for example, than about all the other games combined. And there are more versions of video poker than there are books about the subject! The rules of these games, and how they are played, are relatively simple, but the strategies developed to beat them or, at least, cut the house edge, take time and energy to master. But there are shortcuts to learning. As I said in my opening chapter, you do not have to know how the combustion engine works in order to drive a car. Likewise, you do not have to know the dense amount of information on these games to be able to play them with some efficiency, enjoyment, and élan. Just follow my advice!

Blackjack

Blackjack is the most popular casino table game. It became so in the late 1960s, in large part due to the publication of one book, Ed Thorp's *Beat the Dealer*. Blackjack wrested the laurels from craps, when Thorp showed that people who played their cards right—and *counted* them!—could get a slight edge over the house. Has such a revelation been devastating to the casinos? No. On the contrary, of the 53 million Americans who make more than 350 million casino visits each year, there are only 1,100 known card counters! That is approximately one card counter for every 53 thousand casino players. (I got these statistics from AGA President Frank Fahrenkopf at the Global Gaming Expo in September of 2002 and from the Griffin Agency, the detective agency that is responsible for "protecting" the casinos against the big bad card counters.) Indeed, for the millions of players out there, blackjack is a game that sucks their bankrolls dry and leaves them wondering why they aren't winning.

The answer to that query is easy as 1-2-3:

1. The skill level necessary to actually beat blackjack requires dedication, hard work, and a large bet-to-bankroll ratio to withstand the swings of Lady Luck.

2. Most people have never learned the correct—or even *close to correct*—strategy for the play of their hands against all dealer upcards; rather, they rely on instinct and intuition in making their playing decisions—with disastrous results.

3. Not all blackjack games are created equal; some are better than others. Many players have no idea which games are which.

This section on blackjack will explain how the game is played and offer you a very simple, yet very powerful, 13-step generic strategy that can be memorized by most people in less than 10 minutes. If not, you can make a photocopy of the complete basic strategy and take it with you to the casino! I will also apprise you of which games are the best games at which to play this strategy. But here is a hint: games that are good for card counters are not always good for basic strategy players. In fact, games that are good for card counters are also good for casinos. I will explain why a little further on.

How the Game Is Played

The objective of blackjack is to beat the dealer; it is not, as some booklets contend, to try to get to 21. Beating the dealer could be having a hand which is 21 or less that is higher than the dealer's hand, or it can mean that the player stood on his hand (21 or less) and the dealer subsequently busted, in short, she went over 21. The edge the casino gets at blackjack is related to one major fact: if the player busts and then the dealer subsequently busts, the player still loses. The fact that the player has to play his hand out first gives the casino the advantage.

At blackjack, number cards have their face value and face cards are worth 10. Aces can be worth either 1 or 11. Hands where the Ace can be used as either 1 or 11 are called *soft hands*. All other hands are called *hard hands*. Thus A:4, A:5, and A:6 are, respectively, *soft* 15, 16, and 17, while 10:5, 10:6, and 10:7 are, respectively, *hard* 15, 16, and 17. Soft hands become hard hands when the Ace must be valued as one. If a player has an A:6 and receives a 10, the player now has a hard hand of 17.

The game begins with the dealer giving each player and herself two cards; one of the dealer's cards is face up and one is face down. Pitch games, that is, games that are dealt from a dealer's hand, are usually dealt face down to the players; while games where the dealer deals from a box (called "shoe games") that holds the cards are usually dealt face up. When cards are dealt face up, the players are not allowed to touch them. Once every player has his or her two cards, they are faced with several strategy choices and options. How you play your cards utilizing these options and choices goes a long way to determining just how well or poorly you will do at blackjack.

Choice # 1: After seeing his first two cards, the player can take a *hit* and receive another card. You do this in pitch games by scratching your cards against the layout. In face-up games, you simply point to your cards to indicate you want a hit. Some players like to point and say, "Hit." A player can hit as many times as he wants, as long as he doesn't go over 21.

Choice # 2: The player can *stand,* which means that he is satisfied with his hand and does not want any more cards. In pitch games, you stand by tucking your cards under the chips that you've bet. In face-up games, you simply wave your hand over the cards to indicate: "No more." You can stand on your first two cards or anytime after taking a hit that doesn't "bust" you.

Choice # 3: The player can *double down,* which means putting up an extra bet *equal to* or *lower than* his original bet. The player will then get only one card on the hand. This is a very valuable option for the player who uses it correctly as it usually gets money out on the table in player-favorable situations. In pitch games, you turn over your cards and put up the extra bet. In face-up games, you just put up the extra bet.

Choice # 4: If a player receives a pair, he can opt to *split* them by putting up a bet that is equal to his original bet. The dealer will then deal him a card on each hand and the player will play each hand separately. A pair of Aces can only receive one card on each Ace, but all other pairs may be hit as many times as the player wishes. In pitch games, you turn over your cards and put up the extra bet. In face-up games, you just put up the extra bet. In some cases, such as 5:5, the dealer will ask if you want to double or split. If you do not think the dealer understands what you want to do, just say it out loud.

Choice # 5: Many casinos will allow players to *re-split* pairs. Thus, if you have two 6s, split them and receive another 6 on the first hand, you may split this hand as well. Some casinos will allow you to split like cards up to three or four times. With each split, however, you must put up another bet equal to your original bet.

Choice # 6: The player can *double down after splitting pairs.* The procedure for this is the same as for doubling on the original two cards. Once you split your pair and receive a second card on one of the splits, you may place an additional bet that is equal to or smaller than your original bet and indicate that you want to double. The dealer will then give you only one card.

Choice # 7: If the dealer shows an Ace, players can take *insurance* by placing a bet up to one-half the size of the original bet in the playing area marked *insurance*. This bet is a side bet that the dealer has a blackjack and is paid off at two to one. It's a sucker bet with a very high house edge and should never be made.

Choice # 8: *Some* casinos allow you to *surrender* your two-card hand without playing it out. You give up half your bet. Only if the dealer turns over a blackjack, do you lose the entire bet. Utilized properly, surrender is a good option for the player. Very few casinos offer it, however.

The options I just listed are the most commonly found in casinos and on the Internet. However, many casinos also offer other options to their players, or limit the exercise of certain options. Not all casinos have surrender, many casinos will not let you split more than once, and some casinos restrict which hands you can double down on. The more restrictions, the worse the game. It is always wise to check the rules of the game you are about to play. Here are some new options that casinos have incorporated into their blackjack games.

Multiple-Action Blackjack: You get the opportunity to play three separate hands against the dealer's face-up card—each with its own bet. The player must play all his hands first. If he busts any one hand, he loses all three hands. If the player has not busted, the dealer now gives himself a different hole card for each player hand. This option is not good for anyone other than a card counter. Basic strategy players want to play fewer hands, not more!

Over-Under 13: This is a side bet that the total of your first two cards will be either over 13 or under 13. If the total is 13, you lose. Thus, a player betting the over 13 option wins when his first two cards total 14 or more, and loses if his total is 13 or less. The player betting the under 13 option wins if his hand is 12 or less and loses if it is 13 or more; this is another option that heavily favors the casino.

Red or Black: This is a side bet that the dealer's upcard will be either red or black. If you win, you are paid even money. If the upcard is a two, it is a push. Skip it.

Bonus Hands: Some casinos will offer bonuses for certain hands. Sometimes these bonuses are only available if you put up a side bet. If you have to put up a side bet, remember the rule about side bets. Do not make them!

Five Card 21: If your hand totals 21 with five cards, you receive a bonus.

Six Card Winner: If your hand totals 21 or less with six cards, you are an automatic winner.

6-7-8 Bonus: If your hand totals 21 composed of 6-7-8 of the same suit, you are paid a bonus, often two to one.

7-7-7 Bonus: If your hand totals 21 composed of 7-7-7 of the same suit, you are paid a bonus, often three to two.

Suited Blackjack: Some casinos offer a bonus if your blackjack is composed of an Ace and Jack of the same suit. Usually, a specific suit is designated—say, the Ace and Jack of spades.

The Number of Decks: You will find single, double, four, six, and eight-deck games. Given *standard* rules, the fewer the decks the better for the player. I will have more to say later about how the casinos have monkeyed with the rules of blackjack.

Soft 17: All casinos have the dealer hit and stand according to a set of rules. The dealer will hit anything that is 16 or less and stand on anything that is 17 or more. The one exception is the hand of soft 17 (A:6). Some casinos have their dealers hit soft 17 and some casinos have their dealers stand on soft 17. If they stand on soft 17 it is better for the players; if they hit on soft 17 it is better for the casinos.

Royal Match 21: This blackjack option can be found at some casinos and usually has a house edge of between 3.8 percent and 6.67 percent, depending on the payoff scale and the number of decks in use. The objective of Royal Match 21 is to guess whether the first two cards that you are dealt will be of the same suit. If you receive any two suited cards, you are paid off at 3 to 1 (or 5 to 2 in some casinos), and, if you receive a King-Queen of the same suit, you are paid off at 10 to 1 (or 25 to 1 in casinos offering the 5 to 2 variation). Before the dealer deals out the cards, the player must place a regular blackjack bet and a Royal Match side bet. The dealer will then deal to the players. The Royal Match side bet is paid off or collected before the players play their individual hands. Once this is done, the players then play out their blackjack hands. This is another bad option for the players. However, playing at a table that offers Royal Match is a great idea—as long as you refrain from making the bet—as the game tends to be somewhat slower when people are making this side bet.

Jackpot Blackjack: You put up a $1 side bet in order to be eligible for the jackpot, which can be won by making a certain type of incredibly long-shot hand. Like all side bets, it has a tremendous house edge and should be avoided.

Good Games and Bad Games

Casinos want to make money from every game they offer. At blackjack, casinos can make money by limiting the options of the players or by getting the players to play as many decisions as possible during the course of play—or both. Casinos that offer good rules, and thus a low house edge, must get in approximately 60 to 80 hands per hour to make the game really pay off. They do this by going deep into the deck or shoe before they shuffle. Remember—the time the dealer takes to shuffle is, for the casino, wasted time. Many casinos have now gone to automatic shufflers, some of which continually shuffle the decks, in order to increase the number of hands the players play in a given amount of time. Deeply dealt decks and noncontinuous automatic shufflers, however, are great for those 1,100 or so card counters who get to see more cards more often. In fact, for a card counter, "penetration"—that is, how deeply a dealer goes into a deck—is usually far more important than this or that rule variation. And playing heads-up versus the dealer is to be prized. Deep games make more money for the casino and more money for the expert player, but they cost the basic strategy player dearly and they demolish the poor players who are, unfortunately, legion.

As a basic strategy player, you want just the opposite of what card counters want. You want to play at *crowded* tables (fewer hands played) with good rules—dealer stands on soft 17, surrender, double on any first two cards, double after splits, re-splitting several times—and *shallow* penetration. Your motto should be: "Let the dealer shuffle!" Avoid, if you can, all automatic shuffling machines. If you cannot, then only play three of every four hands, as most shufflers increase the number of hands played by about 20 percent.

In traditional blackjack, the house edge for a player can range from 0 percent to 5 or 6 percent, depending on the strategy he uses. The following is the simplest basic strategy for blackjack. It will keep the house edge hovering around 1 percent. First look for the good rules and avoid the bad, if you can.

Good rules/conditions for the "basic strategy" players:

>Double on any first two cards
>Split all pairs
>Double after splits
>Re-splitting allowed
>Double after re-splitting
>Re-splitting Aces allowed
>Dealer stands on soft 17
>Blackjack pays 3 to 2
>Surrender
>Bonus hands with no side bet
>Shallow penetration
>Crowded tables

Bad rules/conditions for the "basic strategy" players:

Restricted doubling, usually on two-card 10 or 11 only

No pair splitting allowed

No re-splitting allowed

No doubling after splits

Dealer hits soft 17

Blackjack pays 6 to 5

Blackjack pays even money

Bonus hands require a side bet

Deep penetration

Empty tables

Automatic shufflers

Automatic continuous shufflers

Insurance

The Ten-Minutes-or-Less Blackjack Strategy

1. Always split Aces.
2. Always split eights.
3. Always stand when you have 17 or more.
4. Always hit your 12 through 16 when the dealer has an upcard of 7 or more.
5. Always hit your 12 against a dealer upcard of 2 or 3.
6. Always stand on your 12 against a dealer's 4 through 6.
7. Always stand on your 13 through 16 against a dealer upcard of 2 through 6.
8. Always hit hand totals of 11 or less, no matter how many cards compose them, against all dealer upcards.
9. Always double on two-card totals of 11 when dealer has an upcard of 10 or lower.
10. Always double on two-card totals of 10 when dealer has an upcard of 9 or lower.
11. Always stand on your hands of A7, A8, and A9 against all dealer upcards.
12. Always hit on your hands of A2, A3, A4, A5, and A6 against all dealer upcards.
13. Never take insurance.

The Full Basic Strategy for Blackjack

You can photocopy the following basic strategy and take it with you to the table. Most casinos will not object to you referring to it when necessary. It is a "generic" strategy that can be used at all traditional blackjack games. If you use it, you'll play against an approximate 0.5 percent house edge, more or less.

Frank Scoblete's "Generic" Basic Strategy for Blackjack

S=Stand, H=Hit, D=Double, SP=Split

Dealer upcard	>2	3	4	5	6	7	8	9	10	A
17–21	S	S	S	S	S	S	S	S	S	S
16	S	S	S	S	S	H	H	H	H	H
15	S	S	S	S	S	H	H	H	H	H
14	S	S	S	S	S	H	H	H	H	H
13	S	S	S	S	S	H	H	H	H	H
12	H	H	S	S	S	H	H	H	H	H
11	D	D	D	D	D	D	D	D	D	H
10	D	D	D	D	D	D	D	D	H	H
9	H	D	D	D	D	H	H	H	H	H
8 or less	H	H	H	H	H	H	H	H	H	H

Dealer upcard	>2	3	4	5	6	7	8	9	10	A
A:9	S	S	S	S	S	S	S	S	S	S
A:8	S	S	S	S	S	S	S	S	S	S
A:7	S	D	D	D	D	S	S	H	H	H
A:6	H	D	D	D	D	H	H	H	H	H
A:5	H	H	D	D	D	H	H	H	H	H
A:4	H	H	D	D	D	H	H	H	H	H
A:3	H	H	H	D	D	H	H	H	H	H
A:2	H	H	H	D	D	H	H	H	H	H

Dealer upcard	>2	3	4	5	6	7	8	9	10	A
A:A	SP	SP	SP	SP	SP	SP	SP	SP	SP	SP
10:10	S	S	S	S	S	S	S	S	S	S
9:9	SP	SP	SP	SP	SP	S	SP	SP	S	S
8:8	SP	SP	SP	SP	SP	SP	SP	SP	SP	SP
7:7	SP	SP	SP	SP	SP	SP	H	H	H	H
6:6	SP	SP	SP	SP	SP	H	H	H	H	H
5:5	D	D	D	D	D	D	D	D	H	H
4:4	H	H	H	SP	SP	H	H	H	H	H
3:3	SP	SP	SP	SP	SP	SP	H	H	H	H
2:2	SP	SP	SP	SP	SP	SP	H	H	H	H

New Wrinkles on Old Bags

You have all heard of the saying, "If it ain't broke, don't fix it." Traditionalists and other conservatives live by this credo. In fact, Lincoln once said that the greatest threat to America was politicians and other bureaucrats who wanted to make a name for themselves by changing institutions that worked.

The '60s generation, of which I am by birth and therefore, reluctantly, a part, had a different credo: "Change is good." We have all seen what that credo has ushered into our world. If you work for any bureaucracy, whether government, school, or big corporation, the worst thing a new manager can say is: "I'm here to effect change." It's usually downhill from there. They will change this, that, and the other thing just to be able to say on their résumés that they made changes. Then they move on, leaving a wake of disaffection and disaster behind them—until someone new comes in to "effect changes" in the changes that had previously been made. Tradition is out. Change is in.

So I subscribe to the "change is generally bad" credo, especially when it comes to casino games. Not one single *new* game introduced into the casinos in the past 25 years has been better than the old standbys of craps and blackjack. The new games generally have higher house edges or much faster paces or both—just look at Three-Card Poker and Let It Ride. A game such as Sic Bo is a sick joke with edges that transcend the Big Wheel and Keno. While many of the "new" games are fun to play, they are not usually good bets in the long run if you intend to make casino gambling your hobby.

Speaking of change, the nickel slot machine explosion, which can now see players pouring oodles of cash into the belly of those computerized, mechanical, and seemingly small-denomination beasts, has turned small-fry slot aficionados unknowingly into high-rolling great white sharks. Many of those nickel machines come with very high house edges. Even though the player actually might be considered a dollar-or-higher player on these machines, he is only getting the return of a traditional nickel player. Not good.

Perhaps the worst manifestation of "change for change's sake" has occurred in blackjack, where new variations have been flooding the market—not one of which is better than the old standby. People play blackjack because they think that it can be beaten. No other reason. Yet the tinkering that is going on with the game is ruining it. You might not notice it now—just like you might not notice the lungs of that seemingly healthy-looking smoker—but time will show that the attempt to "fix" blackjack when it was not "broke" actually broke the game.

Tinkering with blackjack's success—overwhelming success I might add—is tantamount to taking a lumbering home-run hitter and telling him to start stealing more bases and bunting more. Why would any sane coach do that? So why are the casinos ushering in forms of blackjack that are to the original game what a chimpanzee is to a human? Greed is one answer; shortsightedness is another. Both are probably accurate. And both ultimately might lead to players not only abandoning the game of blackjack, but also abandoning casino gambling altogether.

Let us take a look at some of the variations of blackjack that are now on the scene, what kind of chimps these games are, and why you would be a chump to play them instead of the traditional game.

Super Fun 21: This is a single-deck "blackjack" game with a difference. The dealer hits a soft 17, but that is not the difference. Blackjacks pay *even* money, except blackjacks in diamonds, which pay two to one. That is *the* difference. This change in the rules gives the house a large edge that is somewhat offset by some of the following rules:

Player may split any pairs

Player may double after a split

Player may re-split to up to four hands, including Aces

Player may hit and double down to split Aces

Player may double down on any number of cards

Player may surrender on any number of cards

Player may surrender double-down portion of bet after doubling

A player six-card (or more) hand totaling 20 or less is an automatic winner (except after doubling)

A player five-card (or more) hand of 21 pays 2 to 1 (except after doubling)

A player blackjack always wins

Michael Shackleford, known as the Wizard of Odds (his excellent Web site is *www.thewizardofodds.com*), has worked out the first comprehensive basic strategy for this new game. With perfect play, the player faces a 0.94 percent house edge. On a *traditional* single-deck game, with standard rules and correct basic strategy, the player only faces between a 0 and a 0.2 house edge (he will lose between nothing and 20 cents for every $100 in the long run). That is a significant difference in a speedy game like blackjack. Without utilizing Shackleford's strategy, you will face house edges far greater than 0.94 percent. Super Fun 21 is super fun all right, for the casinos that is, but ultimately not as much fun for the players. So if you find that you want to play this version of blackjack, make a photocopy of the following strategy and use it religiously:

Michael Shackleford's Super Fun 21 Basic Strategy

S=Stand, H=Hit, D=Double, SP=Split, R=Surrender
S3=Stand/hit with 3 or more cards
S4=Stand/hit with 4 or more cards
S5=Stand/hit with 5 or more cards
D3=Double/hit with 3 or more cards
D4=Double/hit with 4 or more cards
D5=Double/hit with 5 or more cards
R4=Surrender/hit with 4 or more cards
R5=Surrender/hit with 5 or more cards

Double Down Surrender Strategy:
Surrender after doubling down with total of 12 to 16 if the dealer shows an 8-Ace.

Dealer upcard	>2	3	4	5	6	7	8	9	10	A
17–21	S	S	S	S	S	S	S	S5	S5	R5
16	S	S	S	S	S	H	H	H	R4	R4
15	S5	S	S	S	S	H	H	H	H	R4
14	S5	S5	S5	S5	S5	H	H	H	H	H
13	S4	S4	S5	S5	S5	H	H	H	H	H
12	H	H	S4	S4	S4	H	H	H	H	H
11	D4	D4	D4	D4	D4	D4	D4	D4	D4	D4
10	D4	D4	D4	D4	D4	D4	D4	D4	D3	D4
9	D3	D4	D4	D	D	H	H	H	H	H
8 or less	H	H	H	H	H	H	H	H	H	H

Dealer upcard >2	3	4	5	6	7	8	9	10	A
A:9	S5	S5	S5	S5	S5	S5	S5	S5	S5	S5
A:8	S5	S5	S5	S5	D5	S5	S5	S5	S4	S5
A:7	S3	D4	D4	D4	D5	S4	S4	H	H	H
A:6	D3	D3	D4	D4	D5	H	H	H	H	H
A:5	H	H	D3	D4	D4	H	H	H	H	H
A:4	H	H	D3	D4	D4	H	H	H	H	H
A:3	H	H	D3	D	D	H	H	H	H	H
A:2	H	H	H	D	D	H	H	H	H	H

Dealer upcard>2	3	4	5	6	7	8	9	10	A
A:A	SP	SP	SP	SP	SP	SP	SP	SP	SP	SP
10:10	S	S	S	S	S	S	S	S	S	S
9:9	SP	SP	SP	SP	SP	S	SP	SP	S	S
8:8	SP	SP	SP	SP	SP	SP	SP	SP	SP	SP
7:7	SP	SP	SP	SP	SP	SP	SP	H	R	R
6:6	SP	SP	SP	SP	SP	SP	H	H	H	H
5:5	D	D	D	D	D	D	D	D	H	H
4:4	H	H	H	SP	SP	H	H	H	H	H
3:3	SP	SP	SP	SP	SP	SP	H	H	H	H
2:2	SP	SP	SP	SP	SP	SP	H	H	H	H

6/5 Single Deck Blackjack: The prize for bloody brazen boldness goes to Park Place Entertainment for bringing this anemic version of single-deck blackjack to their properties, and heralding it with big fanfare to boot. Billboards actually proclaimed the 6 to 5 payout for blackjacks as if this was somehow better than 3 to 2. Many players have fallen for it, thinking that 6 to 5 is *more* than 3 to 2. It is not. Remember that 3 to 2 is 6 to 4! The traditional payout for a $5 blackjack would be $7.50, not $6. To make matters worse, if you bet, say, $9, you get paid $10 for your blackjack because the casino only pays out the 6/5 on multiples of $5. So a $9 bettor gets his $6 for the first $5 he bet, but gets even money for the other $4 should he get a blackjack. There are no offsetting rules variations as there are in Super Fun 21, so the house edge for this game is about 1.5 percent. This game is definitely not worth playing.

Now, some of you might be asking yourself how I can recommend bets at craps that have a 1.5 percent house edge (Placing the 6 and 8) but damn the blackjack game with the same house edge. Good question. The answer involves speed and the number of decisions per hour. In 6/5 single-deck blackjack, you will be playing about 80 decisions per hour into that 1.5 percent edge. A $5 player can expect to lose approximately $6 or so per hour. At craps, placing the 6 or the 8 for $6, will see you face approximately 33 decisions per hour and you can expect to lose about $3—half as much.

You are better off playing regular single- or multiple-deck blackjack using either the ten-minutes-or-less basic strategy or the generic basic strategy I have given in this book. The scary thing about 6/5 blackjack is how many players have gravitated to it thinking they are getting a good deal. Somewhere, P. T. Barnum is laughing!

Spanish 21: I wrote an entire book about this game, *Armada Strategies for Spanish 21: How to Sink the Casino's New Game!* as I thought it had a great chance of catching on with the public. To some extent it has. Spanish 21 is similar to Super-Fun 21 in all the good rules it has, but it also pays 3 to 2 for blackjacks, not even money as Super-Fun 21 does. To make up for these perks, the game removes the 10-spot cards (although you still have the Jacks, Queens, and Kings as 10-valued cards). You need a whole new basic strategy for this game, as you do with Super-Fun 21. Even with this new strategy, dubbed the Armada Strategy, the house will have about a 0.82 percent edge on you, which is greater than the edge for a basic strategy player at traditional blackjack. Math wizard Michael Shackleford has created a basic strategy that reduces the house edge even further—between 0.4 percent on games where the dealer stands on soft 17 to 0.76 percent on games where the dealer hits soft 17—about what you experience on those abominable eight-deck blackjack games in Atlantic City and in some Vegas casinos. Those eight-deckers are the worst of the traditional blackjack games. So here's the rub: play the most powerful strategy at Spanish 21 and you'll get a game that is the equivalent of some of the worst of the traditional blackjack games.

However, if you play normal basic strategy at Spanish 21, as most players do, or if you incorporate your own ideas as to how to play certain hands, the casino will have much greater edges over you—up to 5 percent! The only way to attempt to beat this game is to go comp hunting, as a savvy player can reduce the number of decisions and increase the amount of his comps as I show in my book. Card counting does not seem to be very effective at this game. However, I will grant that, as new games go, if you utilize the correct strategies, you will get a decent run for your money at Spanish 21.

I have already discussed the various side bets, jackpots, and variations, such as Multiple-Action, red/black, over/under 13, etc. None are worth playing. Stick to regular blackjack; stick with tradition. If the casino you go to starts "fixing" the game, do not play there—go somewhere else.

So keep this in mind, experience shows that new games and new versions of old games just do not hold up to the traditional games and that—let us sing it all together now—*change is bad!*

For More Information About Blackjack

Blackjack is the most written-about game in the casino. There are more than 250 books currently available concerning blackjack, and more are on the way. Many of the books about blackjack are great, many are okay, and many raise the question, "Why was this book ever published?" Rather than take up an inordinate amount of space here, check the appendix for a list of recommended blackjack books. The two books in this section can take you from a novice to an expert player—if you utilize the information given and work at it. But if you want to make blackjack your game, then read as many of the recommended books as you can.

Best Blackjack by Frank Scoblete (Bonus Books, $14.95): Discover which games can be beaten and how. You will learn a simple, but powerful, card-counting method that enables you to get the edge over the good blackjack games. You will also learn basic strategies and variations for single and multiple-deck games. Contains delightful stories about the "Million-Dollar Bum," "The Ploppy from Hell," and concludes with an extensive "Blackjack Diary," that shows what it is like to be a skillful player in the casino.

Get the Edge at Blackjack: Revolutionary Advantage-Play Methods That Work! by John May (Bonus Books, $13.95): Once you know how to count cards, where do you go from there? This book is where. John May reveals the secrets of the pros: methods for getting the edge at blackjack by legal means, such as "the stacker play," "hole carding," "card steering," "card sequencing," and "shadow play." It contains the latest on how to beat the "preferential shuffle," "card readers," and "shuffle machines."

Video Poker

The casinos of America are fast becoming video poker paradises as video poker machines begin to bump traditional slot machines for floor space. No game, be it table or machine, has the sheer variety of playing options video poker has. At latest count, there are well over 150 different games from which to choose. If casinos are evolutionary playgrounds, then the survival of the fittest seems to be going to video poker.

That is good news for casinos, which are raking in the profits from these machines, but not necessarily good news for players who seem at a loss as to how to win. You see there is a snake in this new machine Eden, every bit as cunning as the snake that brought down Adam and Eve. In fact, the sheer variety of machines that you can play is simultaneously the charm and the danger of video poker.

Unlike slot machines, a knowledgeable player can get an edge on certain video poker machines and cut the edge to a bare minimum on others. That sounds good in theory, but it's much tougher to do in practice. The first problem appears when trying to figure which machines are which. Is the Jacks-or-Better draw poker machine over here the same as the Jacks-or-Better draw poker machine over there? Maybe. Maybe not.

How can you tell? You have to read the face of the machine. Certain payouts inform us that the machine is a full-pay, close-to-full-pay, or negative payback, and by how much. For example, on the archetypal Jacks-or-Better draw poker machine, players know to look for machines that pay four thousand *or more* coins on the Royal Flush when playing full coin, while paying nine coins on the Full House, and six coins on the Flush on the single coin line. These machines are traditionally classified as "full-pay" 9/6 machines (even though the casino will have a slight edge on them).

However, you could find yourself looking at a machine that looks exactly like a "full-pay" Jacks-or-Better but not notice that the full-house line has been changed from nine coins to eight coins and, perhaps, the flush line has been altered and is now paying only five and not six coins. Suddenly, a game that was almost even between the player and the casino will be giving the casino a nice big edge.

That brings me to the guiding rule of video poker: *know which machines to play.*

The second problem comes when trying to figure out how to play this or that machine. Beatable machines are only beatable if you know the right strategies to employ. The same goes for machines with theoretically low house edges. If you do not play the right strategies, even on supposedly good machines, you could be giving the casinos hefty edges over you. Now here is the snake in video-poker Eden: just about every machine has its own distinct strategy to employ to get the best return. Make no mistake about this—video poker is a game where skill in the long run prevails over luck. But how is it possible to know every strategy for every machine? For most of us, it is not. Unless we have a memory like a computer, there is just too much to know.

Luckily, however, we live in an age of ready access to expert knowledge—knowledge that even the casinos would prefer you didn't know. There are literally dozens of sources of good information on just about every machine the casinos have planted in their gardens—the beautiful high-paying ones and the stinkweeds. You just have to know where to go if you want to become an expert player.

Another thing that makes video poker so playable is the fact that you can take your strategy—either on a card or photocopy—into the casino with you and use it at the machines. No one will be rushing you. No dealer will be trying to get you to make a quick decision so he can move on to the next player. You can take your time and learn the right moves at your own pace.

There is another downside to video poker that is not often discussed. Like the table-game Let It Ride, video poker has many more losing decisions than winning ones. In fact, you will be behind much more often than you will be ahead during your sessions because you'll need to hit premium hands—mostly long shots—to be ahead. And you will need enough money to play long enough to get those all-important Royal Flushes. So, expect that the majority of your sessions will be losers, but some of your winning sessions will be for spectacular amounts. That is the nature of the video poker beast.

The following strategies are for the three most popular forms of video poker: Jacks-or-Better, Deuces Wild, and Joker Poker. They are "generic" strategies, far from perfect, but they can be used to get you started at the game. However, if you are going to be a video poker player, you really should select a few types of machines to play and get the optimum strategy for those machines from the recommended books.

The Ten-Minutes-or-Less Video Poker Strategy

Jacks-or-Better Draw Poker

1. Stand on pat hands such as Royal Flush, Straight Flush, Four of a Kind, and a Full House.
2. Draw one card to a four-card Royal Flush.
3. Draw one card to a four-card Straight Flush—inside or outside.
4. Draw two cards to Three of a Kind or a three-card Royal or Straight Flush.
5. Draw one card to Two Pair or four cards to a Flush.
6. Draw three cards to any pair or any two high cards (Jack, Queen, King, or Ace).
7. Draw one card to a four-card outside Straight.
8. Draw four cards to any high card (Jack, Queen, King, Ace).
9. If you have nothing, draw five cards.

Deuces Wild Draw Poker

1. Stand on pat hands such as Royal Flush, Straight Flush, Four of a Kind, and a Full House.
2. Draw one card to a four-card Straight or Royal Flush.
3. Draw two cards to a three-card Royal Flush.
4. With Two Pair, discard one pair and draw three cards to the other pair.
5. Draw one card to a four-card Flush or Straight.

6. Draw two cards to a three-card Straight Flush.
7. Draw three cards to a suited Queen-King, Queen-Jack, or 10-Jack.
8. Draw one card to a four-card Deuce Royal.
9. Draw one card to a four-card Deuce Straight.
10. Hold any winning hand that has Deuces. Break up a Flush, Straight, or Three-of-a-Kind for any four-card Straight or Royal Flush.
11. Draw one card to a four-card double-Deuce Royal or Four-of-a-Kind.
12. With three Deuces and any two unrelated cards, draw two cards.
13. Hands with Deuce(s) and nothing else hold the Deuce(s).

Joker Poker

When you are dealt the Joker:

1. Stand with Five-of-a-Kind, a Straight Flush, Full House, Flush, or Straight.
2. Draw one card to Four-of-a-Kind.
3. Draw one card to any four-card Straight Flush.
4. Draw two cards to Three-of-a-Kind.
5. Draw one card to any four-card Straight.
6. Draw two cards to any three-card Straight Flush.
7. Draw one card to a four-card Flush.
8. Draw two cards to a three-card Straight.

When you are not dealt the Joker:

1. Stand with Royal Flush, a Straight Flush, Full House, Flush, or Straight.
2. Draw one card to Four-of-a-Kind.
3. Draw one card to any four-card Royal Flush or Straight Flush.
4. Draw two cards to Three-of-a-Kind.
5. Draw one card to Two Pair.
6. Draw one card to a four-card Flush.
7. Draw two cards to a three-card Royal Flush.
8. Draw one card to any four-card Straight.

9. Draw two cards to any three-card Straight Flush.
10. Draw three cards to a Pair.
11. Draw three cards to a two-card Royal Flush.
12. Draw three cards to any two-card Straight Flush.
13. Draw two cards to a three-card Flush or a three-card Straight.
14. Draw three cards to a two-card Flush.

For More Information About Video Poker

There are only about 30 video poker books on the market, many not really up-to-date or accurate. However, many pamphlets, software programs, and strategy cards are available. Any products from the following authors are highly recommended: Bob Dancer, Lenny Frome, Skip Hughes, Dan Paymar, and John Robison.

Victory at Video Poker with Video Blackjack, Keno and Craps by Frank Scoblete (Bonus Books, $12.95): The most comprehensive book on video poker; more than 150 machines are discussed with basic strategies for all of the important types. Strategies are given in English, not code, to make them easy to understand.

Video Poker Answer Book by John Grochowski (Bonus Books, $13.95): Great question-and-answer format. As with all books by Grochowski, you'll have fun as you learn.

Chapter 7

Should You Go with or Against a Trend?

I know a kid who has memorized 250 digits of π—a number that never ends. His achievement is not *so* great, of course, when you compare him to the Japanese fellow who has memorized 50 thousand digits, but, because I only know the first three, I would still say the kid is pretty good.

Anyway, one day I asked this kid to write out the number of digits of π that he had memorized and he did so. I was struck by something that always strikes me when I see a list of numbers—the remarkable streaks and patterns that occur: a bunch of 1s in a row, weird patterns of 5s and 2s, and what not. As a gambler, I think to myself: "If I were betting on what the next number in the streak would be (without knowing in advance by doing the math, obviously) would I go with the numbers that have been occurring, or would I go against those numbers?"

Gambling and numbers, numbers and gambling, and it got me thinking that I would invite you to do a little gambling, right now, just for fun, on some numbers. Okay? So, I am now going to test your wagering acumen and temperament. Then I will let you know if you are a gambling genius or Lady Luck's fool—this is, after all, a brutal test and we are not going to spare your feelings. Oh, and you have to bet an imaginary $100 on each of two propositions, and you are paid even money if you win. We will be dealing with the numbers 1, 2, 3, 4, 5, 6, 7, 8, and 9. You have the chance to win $200 if you get both propositions right; you break even if you get one right and one wrong; and you lose $200 if you get both wrong.

You are going to bet on the following two propositions:

Proposition Number One: I am going to create a sequence of numbers for you, at my whim and fancy, and you are going to ask yourself what the next number in the series is. Here is the sequence: 2, 2, 3, 4, 4, 5, 6, 6, 7, 8 (?). What is the next number?

Proposition Number Two: I am going to pick the nine numbers out of a hat. No number can repeat. Okay, here goes: 2, 8, 7, 4, 3, 9, 5, 1, (?). What's the next number?

Now, I will give you the answers. I will start with Proposition Number Two. The next number is 6. It cannot be anything else because we used up the other eight numbers. If you picked 6, you now have $100 in your bank. (If you did not pick 6, perhaps you should take up another avocation instead of gambling, like, maybe, cross-stitching, gardening, watching paint dry, or memorizing π.)

With Proposition Number One, did you say the next number was going to be 8? Did you pick another number, say, 9 or 1 or 2 or whatever? Well, here is the answer—take a look at the question. It is a tricky one indeed. I said I was going to create a "sequence of numbers" based on "whim and fancy." Does that mean I am creating a pattern that will continue logically, making the next number 8? Or does that mean I am creating something that looks like a pattern but is really just trying to get you to pick 8 because I know I will pick anything *but* 8? Or, maybe, I am just picking the nine numbers in a hat to come up with an answer. So what is the next number?

You are faced in Proposition Number One with a classic gambling dilemma. Do you go with a perceived trend or do you go against it. Do you pick 8 or *not* 8? There is really no way to tell with accuracy, as you could with Proposition

Number Two, what the next number is, because the information I gave you is insufficient to hazard an accurate guess. So what do you do? Personally, I would go with the number 8 if, for example, this were an SAT exam where discovering patterns is a part of the test. And, you know something? I would probably go with 8 if I knew you were making up the "sequence" because I do not think you are as devious as I am.

A lot of people think the word "sequence" means pattern, but it does not. There are "sequences" of random numbers, for example. Sequence is just a word for the order in which things appear. When dealing with randomness, the "order" of numbers may seem to make sense at times, or it may seem insane.

However, in casino gambling there are ways to take your best shot at betting with the trend (pick 8, pick 8!) or against it (pick anything but 8) by having a little more information at your disposal.

Before I show you the ins and outs of betting with or against certain trends, let me first say that in my little test of your gambling acumen, I made sure that just about all of my readers who should not be taking up cross stitching, gardening, watching paint dry, or memorizing π would get the correct answer to Proposition Two and win $100. That meant on the other proposition, whatever you guessed, you would either finish ahead by $200, if you figured out the correct answer, or you would break even if you did not figure out the correct answer. In short, you could not get hurt playing my game. Likewise, what I am going to show you in my "trend" analysis cannot hurt you if I am completely wrong. But if I am right, even a teeny, tiny, little bit right, well . . . it *could* help you.

Numbers Everywhere!

You look at casino games, and essentially you are dealing with numbers. Whether you call them roulette decisions, or craps rolls, or blackjack streaks, the question remains—do you bet with the trend or against the trend? You won a hand in blackjack or you just lost a hand—do you increase your bet or decrease it on the next decision? The shooter at craps just rolled two 6s in a row. Do you place bet the 6?

Now, all mathematically inclined gamblers and gaming gurus know that in independent-trial games—that is, games that are strictly random and where the last decision has nothing to do with the next decision—the odds remain the same and so does that damnable house edge. Thus, if red came up 10 times in a row at roulette, black is no more likely to show on the next spin than is red (each has 18 possible ways of showing). However, it is tantalizing to think around the curve, so to speak. Maybe there is more information than you realize about these seemingly random games that actually can help you decide whether you should bet 33 rather than 12 at the roulette wheel when you gamble with Little Timmy's college fund.

Here is what I mean.

Roulette

In roulette, an extremely small percentage of wheels are biased, which means that certain numbers or sectors will come up more than other numbers or sectors because of a physical imperfection in the wheel or pockets. It is also no secret that speculation is rampant concerning the possible ability of some roulette dealers to control, consciously or unconsciously, approximately how far the ball lands from its last number. This is called a "dealer signature" and some gaming experts, such as Christopher Pawlicki, author of *Get the Edge at Roulette: How to Predict Where the Ball Will Land*, swear this is a real phenomenon. Pawlicki, a sometimes roulette dealer, tells how he can actually do this. Okay, if the above possibilities are actually possible, and if Pawlicki is correct, then at roulette it is always best to go *with the trend* in the off chance that such trends indicate a possible *physical change* in the nature of the game.

Of course, a player checking a scoreboard and seeing that 33 has come up three times, or that the distance between 14 of the last 20 numbers recorded ranges between 8 and 18 pockets cannot be *sure* of anything. More than likely, nothing is happening. So what? If you bet with the trend and the game actually is random, you have not increased the casino's 5.26 percent edge. You are merely playing the same game you would be playing if you bet against the trend in such a case and no harm done. However, if the wheel is a little off, or if the dealer is a little on, then betting with the trend increases the likelihood of winning, and betting against the trend increases the likelihood of losing.

So, at roulette, betting with the trend is either neutral (you face the regular house edge) or positive, but betting against the trend is either neutral or negative. It is best to go with the trend at roulette.

Craps

Craps is another negative-expectation game that the casinos have set up to be random. Have a shooter pick those cubes up, shake them in his hot hands, and feverishly wing them down the table, where they bang, bounce, and boomerang all over the place after they hit the back wall, and craps is indeed a game that is as random as random can get. If the 6 has shown three times out of four, the chances of the 6 appearing again are 5 in 36—it will always be 5 in 36 in such a case, no matter how many 6s come up in a row. Thus it does not matter whether you go with or against the trend in such a case.

But put those dice into the hands of a careful shooter, sometimes known as a "rhythmic roller," one who sets the dice a certain way each and every time, and lofts them just the same each and every time so that they land more or less the same way each and every time, and there is a possibility that more may be going on at craps than meets the math. Here it might be the wise thing to bet on the numbers this particular shooter is hitting. If he has hit the 6 three times out of four (especially if he hits it the same way, say 4:2), then maybe a place bet on the 6 is called for.

If the shooter actually has no control over his roll, then betting with him is not increasing your likelihood of winning or losing. It is strictly random and the casino has its normal edge on all your bets. But if the shooter has some control, however slight, it is best to bet with the trend in such a case because it has a slightly better likelihood of continuing rather than ending. So betting with the trend at craps is either neutral or positive; betting against the trend is either neutral or negative. As with roulette, then, it is best to bet with the trend at craps.

Blackjack

What of blackjack, a game not made up of independent trials, but rather one where past hands have an influence on future play? Blackjack is not like roulette or craps. If all the Aces come out of the deck, there are going to be no more blackjacks or soft doubles until after the next shuffle. However, unless you are a card counter, you do not know whether the future is positive or negative to your expectations.

So, if you are a basic strategy player who does not count cards, do you bet with a winning streak by increasing your bet on the next hand, or do you bet against a winning streak by decreasing your bet after a winning hand? Or do we increase or decrease our bets after a losing hand? Or do we just flat bet and pray?

Walter Thomason, author of *21st Century Blackjack,* is adamant in defending his research that you should bet with a winning streak at blackjack. This is called "progressive betting" and he has a formula for how to do it.

But what does the math show? And those computers that now rule our gambling lives, what do they show?

Except for Thomason and a handful of other mavericks whose inquiries into the subject I find intriguing, the overwhelming bulk of the blackjack research has shown an extremely *slight* correlation between winning a hand and *losing* the subsequent hand, as winning a hand tends to use up slightly more high cards (high cards favor the player), thus leaving more low cards in the pack for the next hand (and low cards favor the casino). So, if you want to go with or against a winning streak at blackjack, assuming you are not counting cards, it is probably best to *lower your bet* after a win and *raise your bet* after a loss. Since the correlation is *slight*, it is best not to raise your bet *too* much after a loss—I would not recommend a Martingale, where you double up after a loss.

Baccarat

At baccarat it is relatively easy to decide whether to bet with or against certain trends. Here is the rule of thumb: it is always best to bet *against* a trend of *Player* wins, but *with* a trend of *Bank* wins because *Bank* will come up more than 50 percent of the time, while *Player* will come up less than 50 percent of the time (we ignore the *Tie* bet). The house has a higher edge on *Player* than it does at *Bank*. Here again, the correlations are slight, but they are there. Just avoid the *Tie* bet.

The Other Games

Unfortunately, in the games of Let It Ride, Three-Card Poker, Caribbean Stud, and Pai Gow Poker, each and every deal is a distinct and separate decision, often played with a different deck of cards, so going with or against the trend is irrelevant. Just guess then, and, perhaps, pray. Or, better still, just play the correct strategies for these games, flat bet, and play slowly—oh, so slowly.

Those Infernal Machines

And what of America's favorite pastime, putting coins in a machine programmed to pay back fewer coins than are put in them? Do you go with or against a trend at slots? If you are losing your money, do you go to a higher denomination machine and hope for a big win to get back all those little losses? Or do you go to a lower denomination machine and wait for your luck to change? My personal opinion is go low and go slow. Why? Unlike roulette or craps, there are no "X" factors, such as a possibly biased wheel or possible rhythmic rollers, to give you direction. Unless the machine has gone bonkers or has been slammed with a huge hammer, it is going to be a negative expectation game all the way. So for slots, less is best: less time, less money, when you are losing.

However, what if you are winning big time? Do you take the plunge and go up in denomination, figuring to ride your luck into the sunset of a gargantuan win, or do you cut back? In my opinion, you should take one-fourth of your win and give it a shot; but lock that other three-fourths away and go home a winner even if you have bad luck on the higher-denomination machine. For slots, it is purely luck that dictates what will happen.

And the Answer Is . . .

There you have it, a way to decide for some games whether to go with or against a trend: in craps, roulette, and the *Bank* bet at baccarat, you go with the trend; in blackjack, and the *Player* bet at baccarat, you go against the trend. In other table games, you play the best strategy and flat bet. In slots, take it slow and when luck comes your way, make sure you go home with some money in your pocket or purse. Following my advice cannot hurt you; just like the wagering test I gave you in the opener cannot hurt you.

Oh, okay, the answer *was* 8—I am a pattern-finding/ making creature, after all. There, you either broke even, won $200, or you are now trying to figure out which color paint is the best to watch dry. The answer to that question is: yellow butter.

Chapter 8

Containing Emotions and Expanding a Bankroll

Any analysis of gambling games always comes down to one simple (okay, not always so simple) thing—math. Yet the casinos do not spend tens of millions on mathematicians because the games, once analyzed, do not usually need to be reanalyzed, unlike that neurotic fellow who lives down the block.

So what *do* casinos spend tens of millions, even hundreds of millions, of dollars on? Emotions. The casinos hire a phalanx of player-development people, ad agency advisors, psychologists, and interior/exterior decorators to figure out how to best get fools to part with their money, and like it! Players, on the other hand, spend little to no time analyzing the games and even less time analyzing *themselves*.

Emotions cannot overcome math, and emotionally being in charge cannot lessen a house edge. However, emotions can structure how you play the games in order to avoid unpleasant outcomes. Here are some examples culled from my own experience (i.e., I have made every stupid mistake I am cautioning you about).

No one, short of a lunatic, wants to come into a casino and get blown away in a nanosecond, or even in an hour. Can anyone enjoy the following scenario? You come to the casino with $400, bet $25 per hand at blackjack, lose eight hands in a row, figure you have to win one hand—after all, you're due— so you then bet $100, which you promptly lose, then another $100, which you promptly lose. "Gee, sir," says the dealer, "bad luck." Wipe out!

That is an awful feeling, a rotten feeling. It is the equivalent of what a boxer feels when he hears the bell for the first round, comes charging out of his corner, and then wakes up in the dressing room 10 minutes later. "How did I do?" he asks. "Ya got knocked out in 15 seconds!" says his manager.

To avoid the embarrassment of getting knocked out, plan all your gambling sessions with an eye to *lasting*. As Rocky Balboa said (and I paraphrase): "All I wanna do is be standing at the end of 15 rounds."

If your stake is $400, do not make a bet that is more than $10. In blackjack, you can play $5 per hand, and sometimes you will have to spring for $10 or $15 when you split and double. You can rest pretty well assured that $400 will be enough to last three or four hours even under the worst of conditions, that being horrendous luck, always assuming you are playing the correct strategy.

At craps, you will want to make minimum bets as well. If the casino has a $5 Pass line bet, make one and put double odds. Maybe, maybe, go for one come bet with double odds as well. At the height of your risk, you'll have $30 riding on the dice. You'd have to hit a very bad streak indeed to go through $400 betting this way. If you really want to reduce exposure and ensure lasting the full 15 rounds (maybe a whole day of playing), then just bet $6 on the 6 and 8—$12 overall. You will last and last and last—like the Energizer Bunny.

The flipside of getting knocked out fast is that night when everything is working just right: the night where you double, triple, or quadruple your money in the first hour or so of play, the night when you own Lady Luck for a while. Almost every gambler has dreamed about that special night and, on rare occasions, some gamblers actually have experienced it. How do emotions come into play on such heralded occasions?

This way: "Let me radically increase my bets and really take advantage of my hot streak."

If you were betting $10 per decision and you suddenly bounce up to a $100, a short-term dip in your luck could easily wipe out most or all of your winnings. If you must increase your bet in the hopes of riding this hot streak into the sunset, then do so in small increments. Go from $10 to $15. If you keep hammering the casino, then go to $20. But as soon as you lose, say, 20 percent of your big win back to the casino, start making plans to call it a night.

One of the worst feelings of all is losing back a big win because you got greedy. That's the equivalent of the fighter who, in the 15th round of a fight he was winning on finesse, decides to try to out-punch a puncher (Billy Conn and Joe Louis come to mind). Bam! "Hey, what happened," says the fighter in the dressing room. "Ya got knocked out in the 15th round," says his manager.

When you have a decent win sewn up (and I will let you define what "decent" is, but it is not tens of thousands if you are a $5 bettor), make up your mind that you will only allow yourself to lose a fraction of it back before you quit. Remember that the casino does have the edge on just about every bet that every player makes, so a monstrous winning streak is not going to continue indefinitely.

The best feeling in the world is walking out of the casino with their money. It is a feeling that delights the mind and captures the soul. The times that you can enjoy such feelings are times worth remembering. Those other times, when you got knocked out early or late, are times best avoided.

Bankroll

When you are losing money, if you think to yourself: "Damn, I could have used that money for my bypass surgery," then you should not be in a casino, but in a hospital—first for that heart operation and second to have your head examined. Unfortunately, most people tend to mix their "mad money" with their serious money. This is usually fine when you go to a movie. You do not think, "Damn, I could have used the money I just spent on popcorn on aspirin for the headache this movie gave me."

Unfortunately, mixing your play money with your serious money is the single worst thing you can do if you want to pursue the joys of casino gambling. Wins and losses can be for relatively significant sums during the explosively good and bad streaks that you invariably encounter. If the amount of money with which you gamble causes you to stop and think about a better use for it, then that is money you should not gamble. Period. True, you cannot play for sums so small that the wagering of them does not matter one way or the other. Not many of us can get excited about playing penny blackjack. At the same time, you do not want to play for stakes that precipitate a trip to the emergency room. In short, you cannot play with sacred money that conjures images of what you could have used it for, and you cannot play with money that is completely meaningless.

If you play with sacred money, or on an inadequate bankroll needed for something else, you are going to kick yourself you-know-where should you lose it. Worse, your spouse or significant other, your dependents, your friends, and even strangers on the street will be genuinely pleased to also kick you there. In fact, give me a call and I will be delighted to add my two feet as well. The best way to forestall any of that kicking is to create a bankroll to be used exclusively for gambling.

Now, you cannot create that bankroll by saying: "Okay, I'll have two of my three clogged arteries bypassed, but I'll use the money for the third to gamble with." You want to create what I call a "401G" account at your local bank—"G" for gambling. If you work for someone else for a living, then take a small portion of every paycheck, say, 2–5 percent, and put it into the account. If you are self-employed, take a percent of anything over and above what you generally earn in a given month and put it into your account. Figure you are going to need two hundred times your bet before you enter a casino. If you intend to play blackjack for $5, then you will need $1,000—*before* you ever think of stepping foot inside the doors, and only for starters. Some gamblers I know got a part-time job, the salary from which went strictly for the gambling account. I first opened my 401G in the late 1980s, after a disastrous experience in Atlantic City. Since then, I build up the account with regular deposits. If I have a winning trip, I put the winnings in the account; if I have a losing trip, I don't sweat it.

Because most casino players play against a house edge (except for those 1,100 or so advantage players), your account must be continually added to. Just do it on a regular basis. Most casino players who follow this advice find that even though they play against a house edge, their accounts grow; the amount they deposit over time is more than what they lose on this or that trip to the casino. With such an account, you will never kick yourself for having a bad day—and we will not have to, either.

Why Bankrolls Are Important

Let's do yet another mind experiment. Terrible Timmy has two dollars, and you have two *thousand* dollars. You play a game called "Wipe-Out," which involves a flip of a coin.

Terrible Timmy has a rather large 5 percent edge—every time he wins the coin flip, you pay him $1.10; when you win, he only pays you a dollar. The object of the game is to wipe out the other player's bankroll. So, who do you think will win the game?

Short of an extraordinary streak at the beginning of the game—a streak that might never have happened in the whole history of earth—Terrible Timmy is doomed. His bankroll, which cannot withstand even a marginal losing streak, just cannot overcome your bankroll, which can withstand massive losing streaks. Yet, Terrible Timmy had the edge—a *significant* edge.

As speed can change the practical nature of an edge (fast games with small edges can often be more deadly than slow games with larger edges), so too can the size of a bankroll. Very few players can challenge the casinos in the bankroll department. Casinos have huge bankrolls. Players, even rich players, have limited bankrolls. The casino can weather long losing streaks because it knows that eventually everything will even out based on the math of the game—in short, casinos will have slightly more and longer winning streaks than will the players. So why is this important to know? For the following reasons:

1. When you have a winning streak, always take a portion of your winnings—before you start losing—and lock them away for deposit into your 401G. Follow my advice and get away from a winning streak with the majority of the money you won during it. And *enjoy* the win. Savor it.

2. Be aware that when things go bad, they tend to stay bad for slightly longer periods of time than when things go well. If you hit an unusually long losing streak, quit or reduce the amount of your bets—you cannot sustain a losing streak the way a casino can. Do not let your bankroll get hammered on one bad night. Always figure you are playing with two dollars against

the casino's two thousand dollars, so you cannot afford a massive loss. Quitting early allows your bankroll to grow with the regular deposits. These regular deposits will offset, slightly, the effects of a bad run and the thoughts of what you could have done with all that money you lost.

3. If your 401G bankroll has been whittled away over a period of several visits, take a vacation from gambling until you can save up more money in your account. The casinos will always be there when you are ready to resume play.

4. Emotions count. And it is much more emotionally satisfying to start to see your account grow, even if it is just growing with your regular deposits, than it is to see it slowly diminishing or, worse, *rapidly* diminishing.

Chapter 9

Fast Comps for Slow Paces

At the casino in Las Vegas, there were six people ahead of me, all waiting to talk to the host. All wanted to know how much time they had played, how much their table-game play was rated, and what kind of comps they could get. The host was obliging. She dutifully looked up their records on the computer and informed them what they had earned. "Ma'am, we have you as a $94 player, and you've played eight hours in three days. If you want the full range of comps, we ask that you average about four hours per day."

The host's request was not unusual. Most casinos want four hours of table-game action per day (at various denominations of play) for extensive comps, and most players are more than willing to give it to them. But playing four hours per day against negative-expectation games (definition: games in which you will ultimately lose) is a dicey proposition to say the least, and rarely are the comps—those free or discounted meals, rooms, and shows—worth anywhere near what you will lose to get them.

But there are ways to get your comps and reduce your risk, too. In fact, in many cases, there are ways to get more value in comps than you will lose in play.

How can this be? Just follow me and I will show you.

We have two blackjack players who play perfect basic strategy, Mr. Ed (not the horse) and Ms. Jones. Now, Mr. Ed has a real-world expectation at blackjack of $30 per hour. He knows he will lose approximately $30 on average for every hour he plays. On his trips to his favorite Las Vegas casino, he plays an average of four hours per day, for an expected loss of $120 per day.

Ms. Jones also has a real-world expectation of $30 per hour. She also will lose $30 for every hour she plays. She too plays four hours per day at the same casino as Mr. Ed, and she too is expected to lose $120 per day.

At the end of four hours of play, Mr. Ed and Ms. Jones go to the same host, George Smiley. They both ask George for a comp to the Italian restaurant. Mr. Ed is told he can get a comp to the non-gourmet rooms ("We have an excellent coffee shop here, sir.") but not the Italian restaurant. Also, his comp can be no more than $30, his "cap."

Ms. Jones, on the other hand, not only gets the Italian restaurant (Mr. Smiley actually makes the reservations for her), but she gets the full RFB (Room, Food, and Beverage) treatment. That is, her room is free, her show tickets are free—everything is free. And there are no caps on her meals.

Poor Mr. Ed has to pay casino rates for his room, usually $40 to $60 per night, and he has to pay for the shows as well. And all his meals have caps.

How can this be? How can two players with the exact same real-world expectation, playing in the same casino, with the same host, have such radically different compensations? In today's gender-conscious world, we might conclude that George is giving more to the lady because he is enamored of her. Or that Mr. Ed might not be the horse, but his personal hygiene is somewhat similar to an equine's and Smiley finds nothing compensatory in that.

And we would be wrong.

In point of fact, George Smiley makes zero decisions concerning who gets what comps. George works for a modern, computerized casino. The computer figures out the players' playing records and decides who gets what. Mr. Smiley just delivers the message. He is the mailman from EPROM, so to speak.

So why does the computer stiff Mr. Ed and stuff Ms. Jones?

You see, the computer rates Ms. Jones as a $150 player, and it expects her to lose $180 per hour, while it rates Mr. Ed as a $50 player who is expected to lose only $60 per hour. Thus, for four hours of play, the computer expects Ms. Jones to lose $720—enough to garner her the full RFB treatment—but poor Mr. Ed's computer analysis shows him only losing $240 per four hour stint—just enough to be a "casino-level" player and not RFB.

Indeed Ms. Jones is a $150 player. She flat bets this amount time and again at a two-deck game where the casino cuts one of the decks out of play. She only plays at crowded tables with six (or seven) spots filled. She prefers not to play in the high-roller salons where her action will be scrutinized more thoroughly by the pit personnel and where often no one but she is at the tables. Rather, she joins the low-rolling plebeians in casino steerage during prime hours where she can be assured that the casino pit crews are harried, overworked, and not as focused on the intricacies of her particular play.

She takes her time in making her hitting, standing, splitting, and doubling decisions. She times her bathroom breaks to correspond to the beginning of a deal, and when she returns, she never jumps back into the game ("I'll wait for a new shuffle, I don't want to disturb the order of the cards."). She starts her play one half hour before the cards are to be changed (in two-deck games most casinos change the cards every two hours) thus enjoying the benefit of comp time without risk as the dealer goes through the elaborate casino washes and shuffles of the new decks.

In fact, when all is said and done, Ms. Jones plays about 40 hands per hour. Because she is an expert basic strategy player, the casino only has an approximate 0.5 percent edge on her. She will put into action $6,000 ($150 × 40 = $6,000), and her expected real-world loss will be $30 per hour ($6,000 × .005 = $30). However, the casino's computer formula rates blackjack players as playing 60 hands per hour against a 2 percent casino edge, and, in fact, most players do play against edges this high or even higher. The computer figures Ms. Jones to lose $180 per hour ($150 × 60 = $9,000 × .02 = $180). Because most casinos will give back approximately 30 to 50 percent of a player's expected losses in the form of comps, Ms. Jones gets comps worth anywhere from $216 to $360 per day—RFB in just about any casino on the planet!

And what of Mr. Ed? Well, he plays $50 per hand at six-deck shoes in the high-roller pits and at non-peak hours, so he often plays head-to-head against the dealer. He plays perfect basic strategy, but he plays it fast, making his hitting, standing, splitting, and doubling decisions in the blink of an eye. And when the shoe is finished, he'll take his bathroom breaks while the dealer is shuffling so as not to waste playing time. More often than that, he will just jump to the table next to him and play there until his dealer is ready to proceed. Mr. Ed loves the action. In fact, Mr. Ed averages 120 hands per hour! Because he too plays against an approximate 0.5 percent house edge, he is expected to lose $30 per hour ($50 × 120 = $6,000 × .005 = $30). Interestingly enough, the casino rates him as losing twice that. They have him playing 60 hands per hour ($3,000) with an expected loss of $60 ($3,000 × .02% = $60). For four hours, his total expected loss is $240, of which the casino will return $72 to $120, which translates into "casino-level" comps—discounted rooms and comped meals of non-gourmet fare with caps.

In truth, both Mr. Ed and Ms. Jones have good deals going for them but Ms. Jones is taking her deal to the max! Ms. Jones has discovered the secret of maximizing comps while minimizing risk: play the best possible strategies at the games of your choice and play these games s-l-o-w-l-y. Look for ways to extend your time but not your risk.

That maxim—extend time, not risk—can be applied to just about every casino table game with excellent results.

But another maxim works as well. Understand the nature of the games that you are playing. For example, two players are playing baccarat: Alan is expected to lose $57.60 per hour of play, while Bernice is expected to lose $58.50 per hour of play. The former is the baccaratian equivalent of Mr. Ed, as Alan only gets "casino-level" comps, while Bernice is getting the full RFB treatment even though her expected loss is only 90 cents more than Alan's. Why? Because Alan is playing mini-baccarat at $25 per hand, and Bernice is playing the traditional form of baccarat at $100 per hand.

Mini-baccarat is an extremely fast game in which it is not unheard of for 150 to 200 decisions to be made in an hour. Traditional baccarat is a slow game, which can be made even slower by players who take their time dealing and exposing their cards, in which 40 to 60 decisions per hour is the norm. If Alan puts into action $25 on 180 hands per hour (excluding ties), that's $4,500 in total action. He bets a combination of Player and Bank (eschewing the 14 percent house edge on the Tie bet), which gives the casino about a 1.28 percent edge over him. That's a small edge, but it's a small edge on a lot of hands. The result is that Alan will lose $57.60 per hour.

But Bernice is playing traditional baccarat. Let us say she makes a point of playing 50 hands per hour (excluding ties) and she bets $100—on Bank only. She puts into action $5,000 with a casino edge of 1.17 percent. Her real world expected loss is $58.50 per hour. But she is a high roller, betting $100 per hand, whereas Alan is just a "rated" player.

Why?

Because for mini-baccarat the casino's rating computers generally use an 80 to 100 hand per hour formula against an approximate 1.28 to 3 percent range for its house edge (a combination of Bank, Player, and Tie bets) and that's why Alan gets the worst of it by far in the comp arena. If he is rated as playing 90 hands per hour (an average of the high and low estimates) with a 2 percent house edge, his loss is calculated as $45 per hour, not the $57.60 it actually is. Bernice, on the other hand, is rewarded. Her expected loss the computer calculates as $120 per hour ($100 per hand × 60 hands × 0.02 percent house edge = $120) and not the $58.80 it actually is.

There is only one drawback to betting as Ms. Jones and Bernice do and that concerns volatility. Because they are betting larger sums on fewer hands, they will have much wilder short-term swings in good or bad luck. Still, getting RFB (or close to it) will more than make up for the roller-coaster effects of the games they are playing. In fact, in real terms, Ms. Jones and Bernice could be considered as having a monetary edge, as the dollar value of the real comps they are winning actually could surpass the dollar amounts they are losing in their play.

Ask Questions

Before you start playing, go to a casino host and find out what your intended play is worth to them. Ask about the various levels of comps. What level are RFB, RLF (Room, Limited Food), and so forth. Here are other questions you should ask:

As a craps player, am I being judged on my spread or just on an individual bet? For example, if I place the 6 and 8 for $30 each, am I considered a $60 player or a $30 player? What if I make a Pass Line bet of $10 with full odds to go along with my $30 6 and 8—am I a $70 player or are the odds also added into my rating?

As a blackjack player, if I play two hands of $75 each, am I considered a $150 player or some fraction of the total?

For any game I choose, how long do I have to play and at what level to get a) casino rate and discounts, b) free room, non-gourmet comps, or c) full RFB. For example, Pai Gow Poker players usually have to bet twice as much or play twice as long to get the same comps as blackjack players because Pai Gow is such a slow game and has many non-decisions.

Ask and You Will Receive

Make sure that when you sit down, you do not start playing until the floorperson actually takes your card and records your name. You want every minute of your play credited to you. Then ask the rater the same questions concerning bet spreads, number of hands, and whatnot that you asked the host. You might think that casinos are well coordinated in their rating policies, but this is not always the case.

I had an interesting thing happen at a casino in Las Vegas recently as I researched this chapter. I was playing two hands of $30 each off the top and assuming I was being rated at $60 for that effort (I had checked with the host beforehand). In fact, after the first day of play, when I asked the host to pull up my chart, I discovered that often the rater had me rated as betting $30! I explained to the host, then to the casino manager, that I was never betting less than $30 per hand on two hands and I was often betting much, much more—although none of my big bets had been recorded.

After another day of play, I again asked to see my chart (most hosts will let you see the computer screen as they check your statistics—if they do not, then play elsewhere) and I found bets of $50, $27.50, and the like. Because I never played fewer than two hands and never less than $30 per hand, I could not figure out how the raters were getting their figures. Then it hit me. There were times when one hand busted and the other stayed in play. If the rater came by during play, and noticed my cards tucked under one bet but saw no bet in the other circle and recorded that, it would account for why $30 (or $50) would appear as my betting unit. On my third day of play, I rectified that. If I busted out on one hand, I would immediately place another bet in the circle even though the dealer had not finished the round. Then if the rater wandered over, she would see the two bets and give me credit.

How to account for a rater placing $27.50 next to my name? Simple. When I placed a $5 bet for the dealer, I would put it on top of my $30—sometimes I received a blackjack on those hands. The blackjack paid $52.50—two green chips and $2.50 in silver. If I took one of the green chips back to get some red to pay the dealer his $7.50 tip, the rater would see a green chip ($25) and the $2.50 in silver and write down $27.50! If you are playing the comp game, such moments can kill a rating. At that particular casino, I started to alert the floorperson to all my big bets—"Jane, check this out. I'm going for $150 on two hands! Three hundred bucks riding on the flip of the cards! I'm going for broke! Pray for me!" From that point on the rating in the computer reflected what bets I actually was making.

Do Not Wait—Comp as You Go!

Get your comps up front, and do not wait until the end of your stay to settle up. Many hosts will tell you to "charge it to your room" and at the end of your trip, they will pick up whatever your play warrants. My experience has been that, for most players, it is better to get your comps up front—comp as you go—rather than wait for the end. This advice was brought home to me recently at one Vegas casino that is noted for being very tight with comps. I was waiting to see the host to assess what I would get for my projected play (again for this particular chapter) and one other man was ahead of me.

The conversation:

HOST: "We have you down as a $100 blackjack player playing for 12.5 hours for three days. We'll pick up your room and $300 in food for your stay."

PLAYER: "Wait a minute, didn't you say at this level of betting I was RLF and that I could charge everything from the non-gourmet rooms and you'd pick it up?"

HOST: "Our policy is to pick up the non-gourmet up to a certain point. You charged approximately $180 per day to your room in food bills . . ."

PLAYER: "My wife eats a lot."

HOST: "About $498 worth of food, and we'll pick up $300 worth."

PLAYER: "But I lost $2,375!"

HOST: "Whether you win or lose isn't the issue, how much you bet, for how long, is how we decide what to give you."

I then decided to try a little experiment. I would mimic this player's betting level and hours played, but I would ask for my comps up front for everything but the gourmet rooms. Those I would charge to my room. My breakfasts (total cost $20), and my lunches (approximately $40) were comp as you go. I stayed three days and got comps for $180 up front. (When I asked for a comp, pit bosses inquired if I was staying at the hotel. I answered yes, but I prefer to get comps this way. No one turned me down.) I charged $487 in gourmet meals to my room. At the end of my three days, I went to the host:

HOST: "We have you listed as playing 12.5 hours at $100 per hand. We'll pick up your room and $300 of your food."

ME: "Thank you, that's very generous of you."

In fact, by getting my non-gourmet comps up front, I was given $480 in comps for food, while the player I mimicked had only received $300 for food. Whether this stratagem will work at every casino is hard to say, but you cannot lose anything by trying it. So get those comps up front!

Waste Their Time, Not Yours

Always take your bathroom breaks, your "I have to stretch my legs" break, during play and not during shuffles. If you come back in the middle of a shoe (or deck) sit out the remainder by saying: "I don't ever jump into a game mid-shoe."

Always stay for the introduction of new decks, even if you had planned to leave the game. It usually takes about five minutes to do the wash and shuffle, and these five minutes will be added to your comp time. In fact, you can sit through the new-deck shuffle and then sit out the shoe or deck: "I'm never lucky on the first deals after new decks have been introduced. I'll sit out!"

Avoid automatic shuffling machines. These are good for the casino, but bad for the players.

In craps, utilize the Captain's *5-Count*, which will eliminate approximately one-third to one-half of the shooters—the ones who seven out early. Most craps players do not bet on every roll of every shooter and my experience has been that utilizing the *5-Count* gets you a good rating without the requisite time. If you are a place bettor, go up on the numbers when a shooter is on the Pass Line. Your place bets will be "off" but your comp time will be "on."

If you can afford to bet $25 or more, play traditional baccarat—do not play mini-baccarat. In fact, as I prove in my book *Baccarat Battle Book,* a $25 traditional baccarat player has a better expectation than a $10 mini-baccarat player! So go for green if baccarat is your game.

Try to play with friendly and talkative dealers. The game tends to slow down a bit in such cases. It slows down even more when you play with friendly and talkative players as well.

Use the Comp System, Do Not Abuse It

Even though you are looking to maximize comps, do not be perceived as greedy. In fact, do not be greedy. If you are RFB, eat and drink what you normally would—do not pig out just because it is free. There was a time when anyone betting $100 per hand at blackjack was an RFB player at any casino in the United States. No more.

Many Strip casinos now require $150 as a minimum bet to qualify for RFB. Why? Because some $100 players went berserk when offered "free" meals with no caps, ultimately ruining it for other $100 players.

If you employ the various ideas in this chapter, you could very well find yourself with a "monetary edge" over the casinos, or, at the very least, with the most comps for the least risk. If you are going to play the comp game, you might as well play it to win!

Chapter 10

Take Credit Where Credit Is Given!

They have the highest house edge of any machines in the casino. They loom in the hallways and lobbies—brightly lit machines with no conscience, which neither ask for nor give quarter—or quarters, for that matter. Many a player will rush to them and start pressing buttons, hoping to make a quick withdrawal. And the players pay a hefty, hefty price on these machines because no one has ever won on them. No one has even broken even on them. Ever!

I am not talking about your garden-variety slot or video-poker machines. I am talking about those ATM credit card advance machines, sprinkled all over casino creation, that charge unconscionable interest rates of upward of 3 percent on a single withdrawal, often adding fees of up to and more than 10 percent of the total money withdrawn. (Fees? Fees? Isn't the *interest* the fee?) Casino players who use these machines are making the dumbest possible move they can make—dumber than splitting 10s at blackjack, dumber than betting Big Red at craps, and dumber than playing Sic Bo.

Worse, using those currency-sucking monsters is so unnecessary! No *smart* casino player should ever give them a look, much less a mention, when right in the casino sits a flesh and blood human being who will give you money, who *wants* to give you money, whose *job* is to give you money, for free—with *no interest* and *no fees*—and will also give you anywhere from 7 to 45 days to pay it all back.

Now, casino players cannot ask for anything better than that (other than a win). I am talking about casino credit.

Every casino has a credit department whose sole reason for existing is to give away money. (Okay, do not be naïve. They give it away in the hopes that you lose it in the casino.) The upsides to getting casino credit are numerous. The downsides are small.

The first benefit to a casino credit line is that you do not have to carry wads of cash when you travel by car, bus, train, or plane to your favorite casino venue.

The second benefit to credit is that the money you have in your gambling bank account (your 401G) can sit there for up to six weeks gaining interest before you have to pay back the casino. If you win, you pay back your marker immediately. If you lose, the casino takes it out of your account. Contrast this with those awful credit card advance machines that immediately dock your account and rip their pound of interest flesh from your economic carcass as well.

A third, generally unspoken, unpublicized benefit to getting casino credit has to do with how the casino sees you once you have, use, and pay back a credit line. Although I could get no casino executives to state for the record that "credit players" are viewed in a more favorable light than "money players," they are. The casino assumes that credit players are willing to lose the amount of their credit line (which may or may not be true). A simple "mind experiment" can prove this.

Two players enter a game and both cash in for $1,000. Joe gives cash and Joan takes out a $1,000 marker against her credit line of $10,000. Both Joe and Joan now lose their $1,000 in short order. Who would you bet on to go for a second $1,000—Joe, the cash player, or Joan with the $10,000 line? I pick Joan because I know (or think I know) that she has $10,000 in "play money" she is willing to gamble. I have no idea how much Joe has. For all I know, that $1,000 was for his kid's braces, and he is in a powerful lot of trouble when his wife, Big Gert, finds out that little Loretta is still going to resemble Bugs Bunny when she hits junior high next year.

Casinos also think that "credit players" are more *motivated* players, which is probably true. My experience tells me that credit players tend to come to casinos more frequently than other players. Casinos like that. Interestingly enough, between 4 and 10 percent of table game players have established credit lines and anywhere from 15 to 30 percent of the table game drop in Atlantic City, at least, comes from these players. Casinos that attract big action tend to have more "credit" players than casinos that attract small to moderate action.

Even more interesting, only about 1 to 2 percent of slot players have established credit. Why so few? Because many slot players do not know that credit exists for them as well. It does. In the future, you are going to see a "big push" to get credit for slot players.

How to Get Credit in a Casino

Just call your favorite casino and ask them to send you a credit application. Most casinos in a given venue use similar forms. In Vegas, the forms tend to be modest. They ask for your name, address, phone, social security number, and the bank account you want to use for your credit line. Atlantic City desires more information. Most casinos there want to know your full name, address, phone number, where you work or if you are self-employed, your yearly income, your outstanding indebtedness, the name of your bank, and the account you want to write your markers against. Some Atlantic City casinos go one step further and ask to know your net worth.

Then you sign a release form which allows the casino's credit checkers to make sure you have enough money in the specified account to pay back the credit you request. This is an important item. When you apply, make sure you have *more than enough* in one account to fully cover the entire line of credit you want! The casinos then do a credit check to make sure you are a good risk. The whole process takes about a week.

What are your chances of being turned down? Stated one casino credit manager who wished to remain nameless: "I'd say that approximately three-fourths of the people who ask for credit get it. The only area where there might be some difference of opinion between us and the patron is on how much credit we should give. First-time credit applications are often for sums that we feel might be a little too high. If someone asks for $10,000, we might say, 'Let us give you $5,000 and we can readjust that figure in the future.' The people we turn down are usually people who just have a history of not paying their bills. Remember, we're giving a loan for up to six weeks with no interest and we want to make sure we're going to get that money back."

What percentage of the money borrowed by players is not returned? The figure varies from casino to casino and state to state, and is a closely guarded secret, but I estimate that less than 3 percent of the total money borrowed by credit players is not paid back in a timely fashion.

How to Take a Marker

Once your credit is approved, your next trip to the casino will probably see you take out your first "marker." A marker is a promissory note that can be drawn directly against your bank account. In fact, it looks like an oversized generic check.

Once you are at the table of your choice, say to the dealer: "I'd like to take out a marker, please." The floorperson will be called over and he or she will ask you, "For how much?" Once you tell the floorperson how much you want, you will be asked for your player's card. In such a case, the casino floorperson will fill out most of the information on a marker form and ask you to sign it. If you do not hand in a player's card, or if the casino is very busy, the floorperson will give you a small sheet of paper where you write your name, address, phone number, the name of your bank, and how much you want to take out. Then you will sign your name.

It usually takes two to five minutes for the marker to arrive. When it does, you will sign it and the floorperson will put it on the table and the dealer will count out the appropriate number of chips (credit players in Las Vegas will get the chips even before the marker arrives). Slot players will usually do their transactions at the cashier's cage.

That is it; you are in the game—faster than with the ATMs and cheaper, too.

Paying the Piper

How and when you pay back your marker is a product of luck at the tables or machines. It is customary to pay back all the money you borrowed at the end of your trip if you won. Not paying after a winning stay, "walking with the chips," is considered a very bad thing. Casinos frown upon players who "walk" because they feel (rightly) that not only have you won money from them at the tables (fair and square), but you have taken a loan that will get you interest for however long it sits in your account before the marker is redeemed (unfair and not square). Some high-rolling, self-employed business folk have attempted to use their casino credit lines as short-term business loans at no interest. If casinos discover you doing this, they will not only cut off your credit, they will say bad things about you behind your back—and you will never get credit at other casinos once the word gets out that you are a "walker." So, never walk with the chips.

How much time do casinos give you to pay the piper? If you borrowed up to $1,000, you usually have seven days to pay up; if you borrowed between $1,001 and $5,000, 14 days; and if you borrowed $5,001 or more, between 30 and 45 days. Each state has slightly different timetables, but this is representative.

But what if you borrowed $1,001 and only (only?) lost $500 of it? Here, you have a choice. You can pay back the $500 you have left and wait two weeks to pay back the rest, or you can simply write a check for the full $1001 on the spot. Some casinos want first-time credit players to do this until it is firmly established that they are not risks.

Why Casinos Give Credit

We know why players would want to get credit, but why would casinos want to give it? Some players believe that casinos give out credit as a part of a plot to get them to play for bigger money than they can afford and for longer periods of time than they should. Although this is not the reason casinos give out credit, it is a pitfall players should be aware of and is the one big downside to casino credit. Your credit line should be in keeping with your budget. Do not take out a $10,000 credit line if you are a $5 player with a gambling bankroll of $500. The temptation to plunge into your credit line for more might just prove too great to resist on a bad day or night.

Casinos give out credit as a customer service, a loyalty inducer, and a convenience. Players should be aware that markers are money in the bank—your bank—and while they are interest free, they are not obligation free. Should you lose in the casino, you will be expected to pay back what you borrowed. Make sure you can afford to do so.

However, given the alternatives of carrying wads of cash and/or borrowing from those Shylock ATMs, establishing casino credit is the intelligent way to go.

Chapter 11

Some Tips on Tipping

There is a great scene in the movie *My Cousin Vinny* when Brooklyn born and bred Vinny (played to perfection by Joe Pesci) visits his nephew in a southern prison. As the jailer opens the cell door, Vinny takes out a wad of bills, pries a few loose, and tips him. The jailer looks puzzled as Vinny struts into the cell. If you are Brooklyn Italian (as I partially am), that scene brings it home. The big shots of the neighborhood were always tipping. As a kid I packaged groceries in a store and also delivered medicines for the druggist. I loved it when I packaged for a Vinny type or delivered medicine to a Vinny house—the tips were enormous. Tipping was a sign of manhood in my Brooklyn world. The bigger a man tipped, the bigger his . . . well, you get the picture. In fact, my upbringing gave me the credo: "When in doubt, tip!" The philosophical first principle of a Vinny is "I tip therefore I am—you got a problem wit dat?"

Now, some people are cheap, they do not tip anyone or they chisel on the tips. They are the *unVinnys* of the world. I know one guy who eats a special in Las Vegas every day that costs a mere 77 cents. He puts $1.00 on the table and snorts: "I just gave you a 30 percent tip, honey! Keep the change!" None of the waitresses find that the least funny, but he roars with laughter when he says it. Having worked as a waiter in my youth, I know the labor that goes into feeding the multitudes and the sinking feeling that if they do not tip, you do not make a living.

Some jobs are structured in such a way that the tips are the main economic incentive for doing them. Waiters and waitresses rarely make minimum wage as their base pay—if you do not tip them, they do not eat. Casino-hotel workers rely on tips to make a living as well. The blackjack dealer you hear talking about her husband, her family, and her house makes minimum wage or, in some of the high-end places, slightly better than minimum wage. If you do not tip her, she will have to find other employment. The fact of the matter is that service industry workers need tips to live. In a very real way, they are working for you and you pay their wages.

Needless to say, I am not one of those gaming writers who says, "Never tip anyone in a casino-hotel. The casinos have the edge so why give them more money?" You are not tipping the casino. You are tipping a person who is doing you a service. I realize that some advantage-players do not tip for fear such tips take away from their edge. Too bad. If you are not a good enough player to figure in a few bucks for the dealer in your advantage calculations, then maybe you should consider another avocation such as, oh, memorizing digits of π.

Do not be cheap. Do not be an unVinny. If the individual is giving good, professional service—from barber to bell-hop, dealer to doorman—then tip him or her. That tip tells them what a good job they are doing. Do not be Scrooge. That tip might be for Tiny Tim's operation!

Of course, if the worker has the personality of Attila the Hun; if he or she is mean, nasty, disdainful, or smelly, then by all means "stiff 'em." "Stiffing" tells them what an awful job they are doing and that maybe they should get a different kind of job, such as composing symphonies or discovering cures for cancer.

My personal experience in casino-hotels has been almost universally good so you will not find many "stiffs" among the non-dealing personnel. And only on rare occasions will you find a dealer who should be dealt with harshly.

So what should you tip the various people whose hands will be extended in friendship? Here's my formula:

- Valet parkers should get $2 to $3 when they retrieve your car.
- Bellhops should get $1 to $2 per piece of luggage lugged to room or car.
- Waiters and waitresses should get 20 percent of the pre-tax check if they are friendly and professional. If they are cold and professional, give them 15 percent. If they are disdainful give them 10 percent.
- Maître d's in swanky restaurants that bring you to your table and give you the wine list—I will leave this up to you.
- Dealers should be tipped by putting up a bet for them. There is no law that says what a dealer's tip should be, and no rule of thumb, either, as there is with waiters and waitresses. A few bucks from a red chip player, a few reds from a green chip player, a few more reds, maybe even a green, for a black and purple chip player, every 20 minutes to 40 minutes would be generous.
- I do not know why, but when you win an epic jackpot, the person who pays it to you, usually the change person, generally expects a tip. Follow your instincts here. "Luckily," I have never had to worry about this because I have yet to win an epic jackpot—or a non-epic jackpot, for that matter.
- If you work out in the spa, it is customary to leave a tip if the attendants have been attending to you. Did they bring you water? Did they see to your towel? Fifteen to 20 percent of the spa fee is a generous tip. By the way, for masseuses and trainers, different clubs have different

rules. Do not be afraid to ask: "Is it customary to tip the masseuse?" when you make your reservation.

- Maids should be tipped generously. To me, they have the roughest job in the hotel (my God, they clean strangers' bathrooms!) and yet folks tend to give them $1 a day. No, no, a thousand times no. I would rather stiff one of those good fellows who lead you to your table at a show than be cheap with a maid. Five bucks a day! The problem for the poor maids is the fact that you tip them at the end of your stay in a casino-hotel, after you have (probably) lost all your money and when you are suddenly trying to economize. To avoid that, and to assure really, really prompt service, I tip the maid immediately upon my arrival. I find out who my maid will be, introduce myself to her, tell her I am staying in such and such a room, and that this (the money) is for her. I also make it known that I will tip at the end of the trip as well. An important caveat here: sometimes the maid who slaved in your room is off on the day you leave to go home. You leave a tip and her substitute gets it. Make a point of finding out who your maid is and leave the tip with her directly or with her supervisor. And remember, she cleans your toilet!

Chapter 12

Do Not Fall for Scams and Scammers

The encyclopedia salesman stood at the doorway.

"Don't you want your children to have easy access to a world of knowledge?"

"Yes," said the neighbor.

"Don't you think it is important for the children to have a reference that they can look up when they need important information?" asked the salesman.

"Yes," she replied.

"You wouldn't want to deprive your children of knowledge, would you?"

"No," she said.

"Then you'll definitely want this encyclopedia set," said the salesman. "And we have a special price just for the next 24 hours. That's right. Instead of paying $350, you just pay $250. You're saving $100. But you have to act now."

"Oh, I don't know . . . ."

"Your children are the most important people in your life, aren't they?"

"Yes, yes, of course . . . ."

"How could you ever deprive them of something this special?" said the salesman. "But you have to act *now*!"

The neighbor acted. Fast. She bought those encyclopedias and gave the salesman cash. ("And if you pay cash, you only pay $225—a savings of $125!") The encyclopedias arrived in a few weeks, but in those few weeks the neighbor discovered that another neighbor had bought the same set off the Internet for $150. The high-powered salesman had pressed that other neighbor as well, but she hadn't budged. She too liked the idea of having a set of encyclopedias in the house, but she wasn't going to be rushed into buying it.

That other neighbor was smart.

Most things in life shouldn't be rushed. Take your time selecting your meal in a restaurant, linger over the decision of whom you should marry, or whether to marry at all—and never buy any gambling system where the seller tries to rush you into making a snap decision.

"The Super-Duplex Baccarat System is guaranteed to win you millions! But you must act within 24 hours to get the special discount!"

Or . . .

"The Oblong Blackjack Master Craft No-Count Star System, guaranteed to bring the casinos to their knees, will only be sold to the first one thousand people who order. So hurry, hurry, hurry. This is you last chance."

If some salesperson insists that you should hurry—do not hurry. Be perverse, do the opposite. Rushing is fine if, and only if, a saber-toothed tiger is about to jump on you.

But most things should not be hurried. If something is worth having, it is also worth investigating and then waiting for. Decisions made in the heat of high-powered sales pressure are generally bad decisions. Good salesmen, even for legitimate firms such as your local chain stores, know that by putting a time limit on something, by rushing the potential buyer, the sales pitch becomes just that much more effective. That is why stores have sales in the first place! They know they could sell their items for the "sale prices" all year long—but that wouldn't give the customer the incentive to "rush" over and "buy now."

Blackjack, baccarat, craps, and other casino table-game systems sellers also use the "bum's rush" to get you into a buying frenzy. They want you to think that if you do not drop everything you're doing and buy their products right now, you'll eventually kick yourself for missing out on an opportunity of a lifetime. In truth, the kicking of yourself usually occurs after you've bought the product, which turns out not to be the magic road to riches, but a big waste of money.

Remember what Benjamin Franklin said: "Necessity never made a good bargain." Take that saying to heart and you'll never fall for manipulative sales pitches.

In casino gambling, however, for every table-game scammer, there are 10 slot scammers just waiting to pounce. Because slot players make up almost three-fourths of the casino market today, slot scammers abound.

Ten Tried-and-True Techniques of the Slot Scammers

Here's a trite statement that you probably have seen many times: "If it sounds too good to be true, it probably is." The operant word in that cliché is "probably," as some things that actually sound too good to be true are indeed true: penicillin, aspirin, card counting at blackjack, and rhythmic rolling/ precision shooting in craps.

Still, a whole industry has been built on making promises the salesmen have no intention of keeping; in fact, have *no known way* of keeping. No, I'm not talking about the "to love, honor, and cherish" industry of marriage, as a good 50 percent of the population actually does keep their marriage vows; or the diet industry, where a few people actually lose some weight sometimes before they explode in an orgy of eating that makes them fatter than ever before; or the cosmetic surgery industry where the "we'll make you look young again" can take an old face and make it look like an old face that has now been *stretched* beyond recognition.

All those industries might have some glimmer of honesty and truth in them. But I'm talking about an industry that is built on a lie, promotes a lie, and sleeps with the father of lies. I'm talking about slot scammers, the seedy underbelly of the "gambling advice" industry.

They prey on the ignorant, the gullible, and the greedy. And they are legion.

Not a week goes by when I do not receive mail from some "slot wizard" promoting his or her "secret system" that is "guaranteed to make you millions." A tremendous amount of time and talent, psychology and postage go into these mailings—much more time and talent than ever goes into the product you receive should you succumb to the allure of "living for the rest of your life like a king or queen." (How do I know that? I have bought the damn things! In the interest of research, of course.)

These slot offerings all have many things in common, not the least of which are outrageous claims for "money-making" opportunities. Yet, no gambling writer has ever taken the time to truly analyze the selling methods of the slot scammers, as their outrageous claims tend to be dismissed out of hand. Thus, the gambling public, always eager for information, is never shown just how these scamming Satans actually sucker in their fish. Until now.

With the help of "Connie," a former "expert scammer" who found religion (in prison!), I've been able to delineate the "10 Step Approach" that slot scammers use to break down your psychological barriers to buying their obviously phony systems and expose the inherent lies in their schemes.

1. Soften the sucker with "agreements."

Prey on the greed of your pigeon by asking questions to which the answers are invariably yes. Note the salesman just mentioned. Would you like to live the rest of your life and never have to worry about paying your bills? If you have children, wouldn't you like to send them to the finest colleges and not strap them with costly loans? Wouldn't you like to take care of your aging parents? Wouldn't you like to have foreign vacations? New *luxury* cars? Houses in several states? Designer clothes? (Note all the plurals!).

CONNIE: "You just can't come on and tell someone you're going to make them a lot of money. No one believes that. Why should they? They do not know you from Adam, and here you are offering to make them rich? No, you have to get them agreeing with you, get them thinking the way you want them to be thinking. You have to get them thinking about what money can bring them. You have to first stimulate their greed. As they start answering 'yes' in their minds, you are softening them up. This is like a good jab on a fighter. It softens the opponent up for the knockout."

2. Stimulate the sucker's jealousy and/or admiration.

The second step is to inform the pigeon that you, the mailer, are rich. Explain how you live; the cars you drive; how you're sending your kids to the finest schools. Let the pigeon know that all this can be his or hers as well, but do not yet explain how.

CONNIE: "It's very important to hold up the bait but not reveal just what it is you're selling. But you want them salivating and thinking to themselves, 'If he can have this, why can't I?' Once you've got them wishing and hoping, you have them nibbling at the bait, ready to swallow the hook."

3. Explain to the sucker how it can be done—without effort!

Here, some pictures of W2G forms (for wins over $1,200) with the scammer's name on it can work wonders. Many scammers have pictures of themselves sitting at the slots and/or holding up their W2G forms. By the way, anyone, *anyone*, even your neighbor's moronic brother-in-law, will be given W2G forms if he plays the slots often enough, as it's only a matter of time before he'll win a jackpot that necessitates the casino giving him one.

CONNIE: "It is important that you make this money-making opportunity seem very easy, that you have discovered the way to make money *without working*. After all, anyone can make money by working. You want the poor slob you're scamming to believe that money will flow in without effort."

Many gambling writers (most recently, Bob Dancer) have astutely observed: "Won money is more exciting than earned money." The slot scammer counts on this sentiment!

4. Explain why you are selling this miracle to the sucker instead of continuing to use it yourself.

At this point people will have the thought: "Why is this guy sharing all this with me? Why does he not keep this a secret and just keep winning at the casinos?" The scammer must now give a rationale for why he is "almost giving away" this super secret. It could be something as simple as, "Believe it or not, I'm bored being in casinos and have decided to share my secrets as I will be retiring," or "I hate casinos and I want to help take them down."

CONNIE: "This is a critical moment in the pitch. You have to give a reason that flies. But the pigeon is ready to believe anything—almost—because he is softened up and really wants to be rich. So the reason might not sound so hot when we say it in the context of a conversation, 'I'm retiring from the casinos because I'm bored,' is about as stupid an explanation as I've ever seen, yet it works all the time. The pigeon thinks: 'See, there, he has a reason for selling this secret to me.' The pigeon rarely thinks, 'Why doesn't he hire someone to play and he can still make a fortune?' So just about any explanation will suffice once the pigeon is softened."

5. Reinforce what this "system" can do for the sucker.

Once the scammer has explained his slot system's "power" and all the reasons why he is willing to share his secrets for such a "ridiculously low price," he now must reinforce the pitch by reiterating that this "slot magic" can give you "the house of your dreams," the "luxury cars," the "worry-free life" that the person dreamed about in the first set of questions.

CONNIE: "Reinforcement is crucial. You have to hammer it into the pigeon's head that all the things he wants are his if he only forks over the $39 or the $79 or the $199 to you."

6. It comes with a money-back guarantee.

If the sucker is not completely satisfied, the scammer states unequivocally that he'll send the sucker back all his money.

CONNIE: "You have to make the pigeon think he has nothing, absolutely nothing, to lose by buying this slot system. After all, he'll get every last penny back if he isn't completely satisfied. This also can play on the greed of people who are themselves slightly dishonest, 'Hey, I'll order this, use it, win money, and then tell that guy it didn't work and it will cost me nothing and I'll win a fortune!' Of course, no scammer gives back any money."

7. Make the sucker feel stupid if he doesn't buy it.

Now that he has been shown what this wondrous slot system can do for him, and the fact that he has "absolutely nothing to lose" by trying it, he would have to be stupid not to buy it, right? So now the scammer keeps harping on the fact that this is an opportunity only an idiot, a moron, a jackass, a troglodyte would pass up.

CONNIE: "No one wants to be thought of as a fool. So you make the pigeon think you'll think of him as a real moron, as will his whole family, and the whole world, if he passes up an opportunity like this. You might remind him that he might have passed up some opportunities in the past because he was afraid to take action—who hasn't missed out on something in life? This will push him even harder into buying your slot system."

8. Make the sucker feel guilty if he doesn't buy it.

Now the person must be made to feel guilty if he doesn't buy it. "Do you want your kids to have to pay off huge college loans when you could have simply, easily, and with no effort at all made more than enough money to send them to college 10 times over?" The person has to start thinking how much he is depriving his family of if he doesn't take this offer. He has nothing to lose. It comes with a money back guarantee!

CONNIE: "Greed, fear of being thought stupid, and guilt are the tripod of scammers. If you can get the person to experience all three, you have a definite sale."

9. Put the "bum's rush" on the sucker!

As stated, thinking is the enemy of the scammer. He does not want his potential customer to have any time to reflect, so he has to put a rush on him, again just like the encyclopedia salesman at the beginning of this chapter. "You must buy within the next 24 hours, as I am withdrawing my offer after then and retiring to Maui." Or, "I am only selling one thousand of my systems and then I will sell no more and I'm retiring to Fiji."

CONNIE: "Now that you have him hooked, you have to reel him in. The bum's rush is a standard technique used in almost all mailing offerings, even legitimate ones—a time limit galvanizes the will of the buyer to take out his credit card or checkbook. In the case of scammers, you'll rarely be able to take out a credit card, because credit card companies allow their patrons to get refunds on items they are not satisfied with. Those policies are no-nos to the slot scammer, so most will not go the route of getting the okay for taking credit cards. This is one of the best methods for knowing you're dealing with a phony—he won't take credit cards!"

10. Summarize all the benefits; poke at the greed, the guilt, the feelings of inferiority, and then offer a discount for prompt action!

A time limit has been placed on the offer. But if someone acts "right now," he'll be entitled to a discount.

CONNIE: "Generally, if a person is wavering, he'll succumb to the discount. He's been softened, hammered, and rushed—and now he gets an even bigger benefit. And the slot scammer's made another sale!"

So what exactly are the slot scammers selling? Dreams, desires, fantasies—pie in the sky—yes. But they are also selling outright lies. Hear me carefully now as I shout this out: *"There is no way to beat the programming of a slot machine!"*

If a slot machine is designed to return 95 percent of all the revenue put in it over the cycle of the machine (*cycle* is the slot term for "long run" when every combination comes up according to its probability—or damn close to it), then that is what it will return. However, the return is never smooth. The machine might return hundreds, or even thousands, of dollars in a short span, and then return nothing for a long, long time. The programming of the overall percentage payback, coupled with the hit frequency, will determine just how often, how much, and what the pattern is of a machine's returns during its cycle.

Slot scammers know that a certain percentage of people will win money in the short run on just about any machine in the casino. If this never happened, no one would ever play the slots. This is how the slot scammers get all those pictures of themselves with those WAG forms for hitting the jackpot. If you play the machines long enough, anyone can get those Wags! The slot scammer just plays and plays and plays some more until he has a sufficient number of the forms and then he puts them all in a collage in his mailing or has pictures taken of himself holding up his forms smirking the smirk that says: "See what I have done?"

And these folks are brazen, too, as are most criminals. One such scammer ripped off sections from my book *Break the One-Armed Bandits!* and sold them (word for word!) as if they were his insights and revelations. His price for photocopies of a few pages from my book? An incredible $99! His thrust in his mailing was that he would show how a person could win "millions" by finding "99 percent return machines" and exploiting them. He failed to inform his pigeons that not only had he ripped off all this information from my book (which sells for a mere $9.95), but that a 99 percent return machine, while comparatively great for slot players, is still a *losing proposition* in the long run!

The fact that one cannot overcome the programming of a machine is not the same as saying that there are not better and worse machines to play or better and worse ways to play them. Even in negative-expectation games, there are approaches that reduce your overall risk and increase your chances of winning and having fun. But that is not the same as offering the public the sun, the moon, the stars—and the winnings to buy all three!

To recap:

1. Do not rush your decisions.
2. If an offer sounds too good to be true, it probably is.
3. Do not buy "systems" that are preceded by high-pressure sales practices.
4. Do not buy if the company or seller doesn't take credit cards.

Chapter 13

Casino Gaming's Best Tall Tales

Did Babe Ruth point to the stands and then deliver an epic home run for a little boy who was sick in the hospital and listening to the radio? Some cynical journalists say the event never happened. Other journalists say it did. I say: *it does not matter!* Babe Ruth is legendary; pointing to the stands and hitting a monstrous home run is something legends do. Mundane truth has no place in the legacy of legends, just as reality has little to do with the field of dreams. If the Babe Ruth story is not true, it *should* be true.

The following best tall tales of casino gaming probably contain equal portions of truth, hyperbole, and myth. Indeed, some of the following tall tales are true; some of the tales are hyperbolic reconstructions of "probably" true events that have been told and retold ad infinitum until their dimensions have become larger than life; some others might just be the products of feverish imaginations. Whenever possible, I have given follow-up information on the tales for further reading.

But whether true, exaggerated, or purely mythical, all of the following tales *should* be true, because we casino aficionados need our miracles and legends, too.

Tall Tales of Fortunes Found and Lost

Honeymooners fans out there will recall the episode when Ralph Kramden, the bus driver, was told that an elderly woman who traveled daily on his bus had given him, "my fortune," in her will. It turned out to be a bird named, you guessed it, Fortune. Instead of becoming a millionaire, Ralph became a bird sitter. The following two tall tales deal with things found, then lost!

The Mysterious Mormon Will

How would you like to receive 10 billion dollars for doing a good deed for an elderly person? Melvin Dummars almost did.

As the tale is told, one night in the early 1970s, gas station owner Melvin Dummars of Gabbs, Nevada, picked up an elderly man on the highway in the Nevada desert. This old man seemed somewhat dazed and out of it; he had long fingernails and a generally unkempt appearance. The old fella seemed to be a vagrant and, taking pity on him, Melvin gave him whatever spare change he had before dropping the gentleman off at the Sands hotel in Las Vegas. Ironically, the old guy kept saying that he was the casino and aviation billionaire Howard Hughes. How could this pathetic, disheveled, peculiar, perhaps psychotic person be one of the richest men in the world?

Strangely enough, Dummars supposedly received an envelope from the old man some time later with instructions to deliver it to the offices of the Mormon Church in Utah, which Dummars did. When Howard Hughes died, the envelope was opened and, lo and behold, it seemed to be a will written by none other than Howard Hughes. In that will, Mr. Melvin Dummars was given 1/16 of the Hughes fortune, approximately 10 billion dollars, for being so kind as to give Mr. Hughes a ride and some spare change.

Dummars might have had dreams of "my fortune," but, like Ralph Kramden, all he got was *the bird*. The Hughes Corporation immediately challenged the will. They brought in a team of handwriting experts who proved that the will was a forgery, not so cleverly engineered by the young Mr. Dummars. Dummars got nothing from the Hughes estate, but he did receive some big bills from his own lawyers.

However, this tall tale has a somewhat happy ending. If fortunes are fleeting, perhaps fame is not, as Mr. Dummars's adventures with "Howard Hughes" became a very popular movie titled *Melvin and Howard.* Unlike the real world where Dummars was considered a forger, the Hollywood slant on the story had Mr. Dummars as the honest and innocent foil of those nasty suits from the Hughes syndicate who swindled him out of his much-deserved 10 billion dollars. In the movies, next to psychotic killers, businessmen are the baddest of the baddies.

Finders Keepers?

What is the most anyone ever found in cash on the casino floor? Well, it seems that $5,000 in $100 bills might be the answer to that question. The "brick" in question was right there, on the floor, for anyone to see. If you never heard the expression "brick" you probably play for relatively small stakes. A brick is a stack of cash, neatly wrapped.

What would you do if you saw such a brick on the floor? Well, the author of the excellent book *Casino Gambling the Smart Way*, Andrew N. S. Glazer, faced just that prospect one night at the Bellagio.

Glazer relates: "As we walked towards the very fancy cashier desk, there was one couple in front of us. I also noticed, on the floor in front of the couple, lying up against the desk, a brick. The couple moved off to the side, and I walked to the window. I put one of my very large feet on top of the Five Large while I decided what to do. Clearly, there was a chance the money belonged to the people who had just cashed in, mostly because $5,000 doesn't get left on the floor for very long in a casino, even at 3:30 A.M. But it also could have been there for a while, because people do not always look down—my two friends were right next to me, and they hadn't seen it—and the place was pretty empty. So, I had a few things to think about: how to figure out if there was a rightful owner, and how to get the money for myself it there wasn't. I didn't want someone else to see me pick it up and then yell, 'Hey, that's mine!' So my size-13 foot helped buy me some time."

Ultimately, Glazer was able to stuff the money in his pocket, and then he observed the scene. The couple started to search frantically through their bags for something. They looked as if they had lost something very valuable. Now Glazer was faced with a moral dilemma of a high order. He had the brick in his pocket. He could just leave the casino, $5,000 richer—or, he could go up to the couple, as he did, and ask: "What are you looking for?" They were, indeed, looking for the $5,000 brick. According to Glazer, the couple looked like they had a lot of money. Would they really "need" the brick? After all, Andy Glazer makes his living gambling and writing. *He* could definitely use the money.

Faced with what Glazer was faced with, what would you do?

Believe it or not, Glazer gave them back the brick. The man gave Glazer a $100 bill for his honesty.

Tall Tales of Big Winners and Big Losers

Tell people you just returned from Las Vegas and the first thing out of their mouths is: "Did you win?" We love our own individual tales of victory, and we even love our tales of woe. But we love those epic tales of monstrous wins even more! And there have been some truly incredible winning and losing streaks recorded in Vegas lore, streaks that start with thoroughly imaginable initial stakes (the kind that you or I might have) and then escalate to wins imaginable in your wildest dreams but unbelievable in real life.

The Greek Bearing Gifts

One such unbelievable streak occurred in 1992, when Greek immigrant Archie Karas, a man who described himself as not caring much about money, borrowed $10,000 with which to play some pool. After doubling his initial stake, Archie turned his attention to poker. At Jack Binion's Horseshoe, Archie defeated 15 of the world's greatest poker players in head-to-head competition, winning millions. In that Karas-ploughed field were such poker luminaries as Chip Reese, Stu Unger, Puggy Pearson, and Johnny Chan. When Archie could find no other poker players who wanted to play him (or who could afford to play him), he turned his attention to the craps tables. His good luck continued, and he won several million more playing a game of pure chance. At the height of his incredible run, Archie Karas was up almost $17 million, and he had all of Binion's $5,000-denomination chips in his possession.

Unfortunately, Archie did not stop playing at the summit of his fortune or at any stage of the descent. Instead, he took the full plunge off the mountainside when Lady Luck turned her face away from him. He lost all $17 million back to the casino. The last time Jack Binion saw him, Archie Karas was sleeping in his car. Archie had gone from titanic winner to the human *Titanic*—only he sunk himself.

(For more on Karas, read Michael Konick's book *The Man with the $100,000 Breasts*, Huntington Press.)

Shoeless Joe, the Million-Dollar Bum

Another incredible winning streak occurred in 1995 at Treasure Island Casino. A man variously called Shoeless Joe or the Million-Dollar Bum (or both), having been kicked out of his house by his long-suffering wife, arrived one afternoon at the upscale theme resort, cashed his social security check for $400, and proceeded to win between $1.3 and $1.6 million in a single week of almost continuous blackjack play.

I personally interviewed the dealers, pit personnel, washroom attendants, waiters, and waitresses who dealt with this man, and they all agreed on one thing—they could not stand him! He was the most obnoxious, rude, crude, and, after a week of hardly bathing, stinky "ploppy" it was ever their misfortune to see win and win and win some more. He was also a terrible player who would hit when he should stand, stand when he should hit, and double down and split the wrong hands in the bargain. But during the week of "the streak," all his wrongs turned out right.

Unlike Archie Karas in the earlier tale, Shoeless Joe, the Million-Dollar Bum, did manage to get away with some money. As the story goes, when his luck turned bad, Steve Wynn, then owner of Treasure Island, kicked the smelly bum out while he still had $40,000 of the casino's money. According to one dealer, the Million-Dollar Bum was last seen in the parking lot of the Gold Coast Casino several miles from Treasure Island drinking from a bottle wrapped in a paper bag. He has not been seen or heard or smelled since.

(For more on the Million-Dollar Bum, read Frank Scoblete's book *Best Blackjack*, Bonus Books.)

Tall Tales of Larger-Than-Life People

Have Suitcase, Will Travel

The story of the "Suitcase Man" is one of the most well known of the modern legends of Las Vegas, and it has lost nothing in the telling during the last 20 years. In fact, there are at least six different versions of the story. I think this one is the most accurate:

William Lee Bergstrom arrived at Binion's Horseshoe with a suitcase filled with $777,000, which he bet all on the Don't Pass line at craps. The shooter established a point of six, and then sevened out two rolls later. Bergstrom took his original $777,000 and his win of $777,000, packed them into two suitcases, and left.

However, Bergstrom could not stay away for long. He came back and won a $590,000 bet, then he came back and won a $190,000 bet, then again he won $90,000 and then (*circa* 1984) he came back to make his famous $1,000,000 bet—which he lost! Three months later, Bergstrom killed himself in a hotel room. In this version of the tale, Bergstrom died $647,000 ahead.

The other versions of the story have Bergstrom only returning once for that $1,000,000 bet, losing it, and heading for his room, where he blew his head off. The maid found him—all over. Other stories have him leaping out of the top floor window of the Tropicana hotel after losing the million, disturbing the fish in the pond. Still others have him poisoning himself or dying from an overdose of pills. While a cat may have nine lives, Bergstrom, the Suitcase Man, seems to have had nine deaths! But one thing is certain, from the research I have done, Bergstrom was up when he did himself in.

The Real Pac Man!

He is way larger than life, a gambling giant who has a bankroll that can dwarf some small nations. He bets in the hundreds of thousands per decision. He wins and loses millions in a single weekend of blackjack and baccarat play. He can level a casino if he gets lucky. More tall tales are circulating about him than about any other high roller in history. He is Australian gazillionaire, Kerry Packer, whose $40 million win at MGM Grand in the late 1990s caused many an eyebrow to lift and many an executives' head to roll. And the myths surrounding Australia's gambling and media tycoon just get bigger and bigger. His generosity is the envy of philanthropists everywhere. His tips can equal a person's yearly wage. In one story, Packer is reputed to have tipped one waitress a house! He pays off her mortgage in another version. In another tale, Packer tips $125,000 in chips he did not want to the dealer at whose table he was playing.

A favorite Packer tall tale has made the rounds for the past half-dozen years in various forms. Here is the one I heard: a loud and obnoxious Texas high roller is playing at the same table as Mr. Packer. This man is being as obnoxious as, well, as a stereotypical obnoxious Texan. Finally, Kerry asks the man to ease up. The man gets louder and even more obnoxious. "Do you know who I am?" he says. "I am worth $60 million, pardner!" The Texan pauses to let this sink in, then adds: *"Sixty million dollars, pardner. That's what I'm worth."* Packer eyes him, pauses for effect, and then says: "I'll flip you for it!"

(For different versions of these Kerry Packer stories, read Barney Vinson's book *Ask Barney*, Bonus Books.)

Tall Tales About Defying the Odds

Most casino players have to take their economic lumps, sooner or later, because they play against a house edge. But sometimes lightning strikes and the oddest things happen—so odd, in fact, that they completely defy the odds.

The longest streak for a single number appearing in succession at roulette is six. It has happened twice in history, once in San Juan in 1956 and once in Las Vegas in 2000. On July 14, 2000, the number 7 came up six times in a row at Caesars Palace in Las Vegas. What are the odds of a given number hitting six times in a row? They are 3,010,936,383 to 1! You would expect that the casino would have lost tens of thousands of dollars on people betting such a hot number. Not so. The patrons continued to play as they always did and the casino lost a measly $300 during the record-setting spins. Now that is truly hard to believe! (Barney Vinson, an eyewitness to the "Caesars' Six," writes about it in his book *Ask Barney*, Bonus Books.)

At craps, the average roll lasts about eight throws. That is *maybe* a couple of minutes. Yet, the greatest "verified" roll of all time was one Stanley Fujitake, the famous "Golden Arm" from Hawaii, who rolled for more than three hours at the California Club in Las Vegas in the 1980s. The greatest back-to-back rolls occurred at the Frontier around 1994, during the culinary strike, when roller number one held the dice for a little over an hour and 10 minutes, and then roller number two went him 10 minutes more! The combined roll of two and one-half hours was the longest confirmed back-to-back craps roll on record. I know this happened because I witnessed it!

Perhaps the longest sustained winning *shooting* streaks in craps belong to a woman known as "the Arm," a now legendary craps player from Atlantic City. The Arm played at least once a week with the Captain, and, according to those in the know, she rarely had a losing roll. She might have had poor rolls now and again on this or that attempt, but when the dice returned to her, she would heat up the table. The Captain said of her, "She was completely focused when she rolled. I'd say her *average* rolls lasted 15 to 20 minutes, but she has strung together back-to-back 45-minute and one-hour rolls that I witnessed. She was a master of avoiding the 7."

"The Arm" was the greatest rhythmic roller I ever saw. I wrote about her in *Beat the Craps Out of the Casinos: How to Play Craps and Win!* She is, I believe, one of the reasons why the Captain's ledgers are *heavily* in the black during her greatest years of rolling (1980–1992) and why the Captain became the first player to realize that some shooters could indeed change a negative game into a positive game by their rhythmic rolling ability.

Bad Boys

Whatever Happened to Holyfield's Ear?

Nothing brings out the crowds in Las Vegas like a boxing match or a good buffet. And, perhaps, the greatest evening of boxing and buffeting was the night of June 28, 1997, when Mike Tyson munched on Evander Holyfield's ears. Tyson found the first ear wanting, and spit it out. But that didn't stop him from nibbling on the second lobe. When Tyson was disqualified for improper table manners, a full-scale riot ensued as Tyson's fans rampaged through the MGM Grand. Gunshots (eyewitnesses) or champagne corks (official report) were heard exploding inside the casino as angry young men dripping with gold from tooth and nail decided to help themselves to various colored chips as they overturned blackjack tables and storm-trooped their way through the casino, occasionally stopping to belt out a casino patron or two who happened to be in their way.

But the answer to the biggest question of the evening has remained a mystery, at least until now: whatever happened to that piece of Holyfield's ear? (From the first and bigger bite, not that second little nibble.) Did someone clean it up? Throw it out? Save it?

Here is the story as I pieced it together from one of Tyson's former groupies, who is currently being held in the maximum security wing at the Culinary Institute of New York. When the boxing ring was inundated with hundreds of unauthorized individuals just after Tyson's banquet, one of Tyson's (perhaps literally) rabid supporters scooped up the piece of bloody ear and absconded with it. This supporter dried the piece of ear and now proudly wears it on a chain around his neck. It is said that he can be seen at Tyson's fights waving it in front of the camera—kind of like a rabbit's foot.

The Greatest Crossroader

A crossroader is a crook. He cheats casinos. But the word "crossroader" sounds almost glamorous, like "highwayman." Carl Sifarkas, in his monumental work *The Encyclopedia of Gambling* (Facts on File Books), dubs Glen Grayson the "king of the crossroaders." Grayson was the head of a team of thieves who hit casinos all over the world. But Glen's personal playground was Las Vegas, and his specialty was switching in "rigged" or "loaded" dice in the middle of a game. There is no accounting for how much money Mr. Grayson took from Las Vegas casinos at dice, he never filed the required tax forms with the IRS, but we do know that when he had a hankering he would steal *entire slot machines* from the casino floor. He would walk into the casino wearing what looked like an official "maintenance uniform," and, with his fellow "mechanics," he would lift the slot machine onto a hand-truck and walk right out the front door! Keep in mind that Mr. Grayson did all this in Mafia-owned casinos that were controlled by even bigger crooks than him. That is either courage or madness. (For more information on Glen Grayson, read John Soares's book *Loaded Dice*.)

Oh, So Weird!

The best types of tall tales generally deal with superstitions, the supernatural, or the completely eerie—or all three.

Eerie: God Is in the Numbers!

All you have to write is 9/11 and everyone knows to what you are referring. It was a turning point in American history and, as such, has been imbued with all sorts of mystical import. Two of these have to do with gambling.

The following appeared in Norm Clarke's excellent column "Norm! Vegas Confidential" in the *Las Vegas Review Journal* on August 26, 2002:

> Was it luck or something else? Lisa and Sal Pipitone of New York City were visiting Las Vegas over the weekend as guests at a ceremony honoring her brother, a 9/11 victim at the World Trade Center. As the Pipitones walked past a row of red, white and blue all-7 slot machines at Green Valley Ranch on Friday, Lisa, who was born on July 7, later told friends she felt strong vibes to play the slots.
>
> Her brother, Don DiFranco, was among six New York TV transmitter engineers who died when the twin towers collapsed. The Pipitones were among seventeen family members who were guests Saturday at the Nevada

Broadcasters Association Hall of Fame dinner, which included a tribute to the engineers.

Lisa, in retelling her story, said she knew what machine she wanted to try, but the next seat over was taken, so she decided to return when she and her husband could sit side by side. They came back later, found her machine, and the two started playing. Almost simultaneously, they hit jackpots. They took their winnings to the cashier cage and were stunned when a cashier told them they had just won a total of $911.

"Lisa believes absolutely that it was a sign from her brother," said Bob Fisher, president and CEO of the Nevada Broadcasters Association.

The second incident might also make you think that Divine Providence was at work. Against improbable 999 to 1 odds, New York's randomly selected daily lotto number for September 11, 2002, the one-year anniversary of 9/11, was— 911. So many people bet this number that day that at a certain point, the lotto officials would accept no more bets on it. Did these gamblers have a "feeling" that 911 would be picked on 9/11? Some people swear that the combined focus of the nation's attention on New York and on those numbers influenced their appearance. Eerie.

Superstition: I'll Drink to That!

The next story comes from a Las Vegas pit boss by way of *Gambler's Digest*.

A craps player at a Las Vegas casino had a very interesting superstition. After he made his third win in a row on the Pass Line, he would down a shot of bourbon for good luck. On this night, he made three passes and was on the come-out roll again. Before he rolled, he took a shot. Then he rolled an 11. A winner. He took another shot. Then he rolled a "Winnah! Winnah! Seven!" and he took still another shot. He then established his point, an 8, and hit it right back. Another shot of bourbon went down. His next roll established 5 as his point. He made it. Another hit of bourbon. Then he rolled a "Sheven," "Sleven," hiccup! "A winnsa," and so still more bourbon was consumed. His next point became a 9, which he hit after a few tries. As he chugged down the next shot of bourbon, he told the dealers to "Pash the diesh." As he began to pass out and slide down the side of the table to the floor, he was heard to say: "Ah'm jush too lucky!"

Supernatural: The Ghosts of Luxor

Most casino-hotels have had people die in them. The older and larger the hotel, the more likely someone took the *super-express* checkout. But the magnificent, pyramid-shaped Luxor has had several people die in ways that management would not soon publicize. After all, it is one thing when people jump *off* a building to their eternal reward; but it is quite another when they attempt to meet their maker by jumping from the *inside*! Which is just what happened *several* times at Luxor. Now, even this would not be that strange; tall hotels and overwrought people make for explosive combinations.

The problem at the Luxor, at least as the latest and least verifiable of Vegas tall tales goes, is that the ghosts of leapers past are still hanging around the splendid pyramid, walking the ramparts in the, pardon the expression, dead of night. Look up when you are in the pyramid; some of those folks you see walking might not be folks at all.

Now, some of you are probably familiar with the lore surrounding the pyramid shape. Supposedly, the "space" inside a pyramid is great for enhancing alpha waves in meditation, preserving food, and prolonging life. Evidently, if this newest tall tale is true, the "space" inside Luxor is preserving at least two or three spirits of the dearly departed, as well.

Two are said to be relatively young men, and one is a young woman. A wrinkle on this tall tale has one or both of the men being construction workers who were supposedly killed during the building of this great pyramid. So, ghost hunters, and any of you who can say, "I see dead people," you have your mission—find out who these spirits are so that they may be returned to their rightful owner.

(An interesting side bet: if Luxor *is* haunted, will that hurt business or help business? My money is that the more the ghosts are talked about—and/or the more they walk about—the more people will flock to the casino. After all, everyone loves a haunted house—they are good luck!)

More Eerie: Table 21

We finish with one of the greatest Las Vegas tall tales of all time that comes by way of Barney Vinson, the brilliant author of *Ask Barney* (Bonus Books) and the novel *The Las Vegas Kid* (Huntington Press) Here it is, as Barney wrote it, and, according to Barney, "It's all true!":

> Back in the days when the Dunes Hotel was one of the glory spots on the Las Vegas Strip, there was always a line of well-dressed and well-heeled people waiting to get inside the hotel's most famous restaurant. Oh, the coffee shop was fine, and the Dome of the Sea was nice, but the Sultan's Table was the town's number one spot.
>
> This restaurant was the brainchild of Dunes owner Major Riddle, who had the room specially built in 1961 for Arturo Romero and his Magical Violins. As each diner passed the maître d's desk, he was greeted by name and then whisked to a nearby table. The room was dark except for candles on the tables and a row

of spotlights strategically located in the ceiling. These were set for a certain number of violinists, and each stood under his own light, serenading the diners with haunting Strauss waltzes.

The tables were individually numbered inside this elegant restaurant, and the table directly across the room from the maître d's desk was known simply as "Table 21." It was no different from all the rest, save one terrifying fact. Sometimes, when a diner stopped there for a meal, he was never seen again. Not by mortal men, for sure.

It's true, my friends, for even thunder and lightnin' cannot be as frightenin' as Table 21.

> *The first to face its cold embrace*
> *Was a local man of fame.*
> *His power grew, but we all knew that nothing*
> *Stays the same.*
> *He stopped to dine and taste the wine,*
> *To have himself some fun.*
> *The music played, he overstayed at Table 21.*
> *When he would leave that fateful eve,*
> *No more his foes he'd shun.*
> *His bones were found beneath the ground*
> *Before a week was done.*

The victim in question was Las Vegas Culinary Union leader Al Bramlett. He had allegedly hired a local man and his son to torch a Vegas bar that wasn't unionized, but neglected to pay them for their work. They drove him to the desert, gave him a drink of whiskey, then shot him to death. Unfortunately, he was not the last victim of Table 21.

Another gent, whose power went across this
spacious land,
Became the next within our text to feel
The Reaper's hand.
He took a chair, he lingered there,
At Table 21.
He ate his fill, he paid his bill,
He said he had to run.
He went his way, and to this day
He's never seen the sun.
Again we see the mystery of Table 21.

Victim number two was former Teamsters boss Jimmy Hoffa. Hoffa had spent his hours at the Sultan's Table huddled with his lawyer and other cronies, presumably discussing Hoffa's return to the union after serving a prison sentence. He took a plane back to his hometown, where he disappeared several days later. His body was never found.

Soon after that, a gangster sat with others at this table.

As victim he was number three to circumvent
Our fable.
While laughter boomed around the room,
An evil web was spun.
For lurking near, intentions clear,
Was someone with a gun.
Outside of town the hood was found,
His life on Earth quite done.
Few things are worse than this old curse
Of Table 21.

Vegas crime boss Tony Spilotro had left the city for a gangland meeting in Chicago when he and his brother were abducted at gunpoint and taken for their last ride. On a farm outside Chicago, they were bludgeoned to death and buried in a makeshift grave.

Perhaps the fact that Spilotro, Hoffa, and Bramlett all dined at Table 21 shortly before their deaths was purely coincidental. Then again, who can say? After all, the Sultan's Table is gone now, and Table 21 is just another relic of a time gone by. Someday, however, the furniture from the Sultan's Table may be moved to another restaurant in Las Vegas. The violins will begin to play again. At the desk will be a smiling maître d', and in the background, you may see a candle-lit table with a fresh red rose at its center.

> *So if some day you come this way, and*
> *pardon please the pun,*
> *You fail to see the maitre d' get something*
> *When he's done,*
> *Don't tarry if he tells you less your blood*
> *Begins to run:*
> *"This table's just the one for you.*
> *It's Table 21."*

Oh, there are more tall tales certainly, but these I found the most intriguing. If you have a tall tale you would like to share, just drop me a line at Paone Press, Box 610, Lynbrook, NY 11563, or e-mail me at *frank@scoblete.com*. If your tall tale passes muster, I will publish it on my Web site, *www.scoblete.com*.

Chapter 14

A History of Significant Events in Casino Gambling

Casino gambling was all the rage during the twentieth century, and it shows no sign of slowing down in the twenty-first. As with any activity of mankind, the people, places, and things of casino gambling fill many volumes. Picking the top events was not an easy task. I had plenty of help from a diversity of sources, many of which I list at the end of this chapter. Just about every gaming writer I asked to contribute his or her ideas was more than happy to help me out with this Herculean effort. Not everyone wanted to be listed as a source, and I have respected his or her anonymity. I give a sincere thank you to each and every one who helped me compile this list, whether credited or not.

I am sure that for just about every event I have included, some reader can make a good argument for why I should not have included it but, instead, have included something else in its place. That's the nature of lists.

In my opinion, every event on this list has had an impact on casino gambling in some way, either directly (the creation of Megabucks), indirectly (Howard Hughes moves to Las Vegas and buys seven casinos), or tangentially (Hoover

Dam is completed). Some of the events have helped to create and promulgate casino lore. Some simply made splashy headlines. But all were big in the casino scheme of things as they have added to the mystique of casinos and casino towns.

Here goes:

[1.] 1900 (give or take): Charles Fey invents and markets his "Liberty Bell" slot machine. This is a three-reel machine that becomes the prototype for all slot machines to come. It is the original "one-armed bandit." Fey's machine ushers in the era of slots. How does it work? Each of the three reels has 10 symbols or "stops." Thus there are one thousand different combinations ($10 \times 10 \times 10 = 1,000$) to be made. The winning symbol, the Liberty Bell, had one per reel on the first two reels, and two on the third reel. Therefore, there is only a two in one thousand or 0.2 percent chance to hit it.

[2.] 1904–1911: Over a seven-year period, William Nelson Darnborough from Bloomington, Illinois, hammers the Monte Carlo casino at roulette, winning close to a half million dollars. He is a wheel watcher who can anticipate with an unusual degree of accuracy where the ball will land. He can also anticipate with a high degree of accuracy where the money will land as well—in his pocket!

[3.] 1905: The first major hotel is opened in Las Vegas. Called the Hotel Las Vegas, it has 30 rooms and an incredible view of . . . nothing.

[4.] 1905–1906: In 1905, Charles Fey's Liberty Bell slot machine and an apron are stolen from a Powell Street saloon in San Francisco. Because there are no patents on gaming devices, Fey tries to keep his device out of competitor's hands by installing the machines in business establishments himself (probably screwed down tightly), but it doesn't stop this cunning thief. A year after the theft, in 1906, Herbert Mills creates the Mills Novelty Company, which becomes the early leader in slot machine development and distribution up to and including World War II. Suspicion naturally falls on Herbert

Mills as the slot (and apron) thief because the word is that Mills likes to cook. Mills copies Fey's mechanism and within two years his company introduces a three-reel, staggered-stop, automatic-payout slot machine called, creatively enough, the *Mills* Liberty Bell. Some experts believe that the Powell Street theft puts Mills into the slot business, a business his company dominates for more than 30 years.

[5.] 1907: Riley Grannan builds his dream casino in the desert of Nevada. Long before Bugsy and Benny and Billy, this lone prophet in the wilderness sees the potential for gambling profit in the great desert of the southwest. He buys land for $40,000 and starts to build "an honest casino"—and a year later he drops dead, proving in those days honesty might not have been the best policy—and never work too hard in the heat. The desert is not ready for an honest casino, or any casino, at this time. But it will be in the future. The life of Riley is a teaser, a prelude to an opus that will culminate with Nevada being the fastest growing state in the union at the turn of the 21st century. With air-conditioning and honest games to boot!

[6.] 1907: John H. Winn creates the modern craps layout in New York. Dubbed "the Father of Modern Craps" by John Scarne, Winn, a dice maker by trade, makes "bank craps" a successful casino game with his innovations. He letters in the "Don't Pass" section on the layout in Philadelphia, and therefore the improved layout becomes known as the *Philadelphia Layout*. It is the first craps layout to offer players an opportunity to bet the dice to lose. Soon, Winn adds the Big 6 and Big 8, the hard ways and box or place betting squares. Winn also invents the 5 percent charge for booking bets, which is called "vigor" and later becomes known as vigorish or vig. According to Harrah's dealer Lori Heistand, "The guy who invented craps must have been really weird because it goes round and around."

[7.] 1910: Nevada outlaws gambling. The temperance and antigambling forces are at fever pitch during the early part of the 20th century and a strong effort is made on the part of the righteous to close down all dens of iniquity. The entire state of Nevada is considered a lion's den of iniquity and, in fact, it is. When all legal gambling is ended in Nevada, illegal gambling thrives. Now, who would not have known that that would be a sure bet?

[8.] 1931: Nevada *re-legalizes* gambling. Legal gambling? In Nevada? Can legalized booze be far behind? Just wait a couple a years (hiccup)!

[9.] 1934: The Young Sign Company of Salt Lake City builds the first neon sign in Las Vegas at the Boulder Club. Tom Young Sr. can read the future of Las Vegas, and it is all lit up in bright lights with BIG lettering that says, "Legalized Gambling!" The town speaks to him and says, "Build big brassy bright signs, Mr. Young, and they will come and *you'll* make a neon bundle." He does, they do, and the desert night becomes as bright as day in some spots—and Tom Young never has to worry about money again.

[10.] 1935: Harold's Club opens in Reno and becomes the most popular casino in the state. This makes Reno *the* gaming destination in Nevada, a title it keeps for several decades.

[11.] 1937: Hoover Dam is completed, supplying plenty of electricity and water for the growth and nourishment of the soon-to-be gambling boom in Nevada. This dam is still one of the wonders of the world and one of the most heavily trafficked tourist sites in America.

[12.] 1938: The Meadows Hotel Casino opens in Las Vegas. This is the first casino with a nightclub in it. It anticipates the great entertainment town Las Vegas would become. It folds in short order.

[13.] 1940: Tom Hull builds the first *successful* Las Vegas "strip" casino—El Rancho Vegas.

[14.] 1941 (approx.): Charles K. McNeil develops the first "point spread" and modern bookmaking is created. It replaces the system of odds that had been used up until this time. McNeil is a Connecticut math teacher who decides that the pluses of bookmaking add up to much greater personal profits than the minuses of teaching.

[15.] 1943: The second "strip" casino—the Last Frontier—opens. It is a full-fledged resort, with 63 rooms on 35 acres of land. Even with two casinos now operating on the "Strip," downtown dominates the market.

[16.] 1944: Mickey MacDougal publishes the very first blackjack card-counting system in his book, *MacDougal on Dice and Cards*. This is almost *20 years before* Edward O. Thorp would turn the casino world upside down with his own card-counting revolution.

[17.] 1944: The first big star plays Las Vegas. Her name is Sophie Tucker, and the Last Frontier Hotel bags her for a two-week engagement. And, in that same year in that same casino, the city's first wedding chapel opens—The Little Church of the West. Talk about foreshadowing the future of Las Vegas!

[18.] 1946: Bugsy Siegel opens the Flamingo Hotel Casino on "the Strip." This casino comes at the right time and in the right place as the postwar boom puts Las Vegas and "the Strip" on the map. The year after this resort opens, Bugsy's business associates take him *off* the map!

[19.] 1949: *Scarne on Cards* by John Scarne is published. Scarne is considered the premier gaming writer of the first half century, and, while some of his strategies have been shown to be erroneous in light of computer analysis, he is still considered a must-read for gaming aficionados.

[20.] 1949: Nick "the Greek" Dandalos and poker legend Johnny Moss go head-to-head in an unofficial world's championship match. The match lasts more than five months, and the two opponents play for days at a time without sleep. All forms of poker are included. Both men exchange the lead and gaze at each other like warriors from behind their walls of chips. Finally, just like in the Trojan War, the Greek wins.

[21.] 1950: The Golden Nugget Gambling Hall in downtown Las Vegas introduces the "center dealer" at poker. Prior to this, players dealt their own cards in the casino poker rooms. This gives control of the game to the casinos. The "center dealer" is now standard in all poker rooms.

[22.] 1950–1951: Senator Estes Kefauver holds hearings into organized crime's association with casino gambling in Las Vegas. These hearings cause Nevada to tighten its requirements for casino licenses. The gangsters are gone, the casinos remain, and ask any kid in America who Kefauver was and he will reply: "Huh?"

[23.] 1951: The Johnson Act passes in Congress, part of the postwar crackdown on gambling. This act outlaws the sale and distribution of slot machines in all states except Nevada and certain jurisdictions in Idaho and Maryland.

[24.] 1951: The legendary Benny Binion opens the Horseshoe. This casino becomes known as the "gambler's casino," as it allows the highest bets in Vegas. The motto of Benny Binion is, "Your first bet is your limit." If you want to bet a million, just put it up right away and Binion will cover it. When Binion's Horseshoe opens, the normal limits at a craps table in Vegas are $50 for the maximum bet. At the Horseshoe, it is $500. When it opens, it is a "carpet joint" because Benny put carpet on the floor. The casinos near it were often "sawdust joints" because they had sawdust on the floor for the guys who missed the spittoons. I certainly do not miss the spittoons, do you?

[25.] 1951: Frank Sinatra makes his Las Vegas debut at the Desert Inn. Although Frankie would go on to become a Las Vegas legend, this first appearance got decidedly mixed reviews. In fact, Sinatra threatens to do it "his way" to one reviewer who says Sinatra had just been going through the motions. The reviewer has to worry about "strangers in the night" approaching for several years after that particular review appears.

[26.] 1955: Harrah's purchases George's Gateway Club in Lake Tahoe, and smart management and insightful public relations helps make Tahoe a great gaming destination. Harrah's ultimately becomes one of the big players in the gaming boom of the 1990s.

[27.] 1956: Viva Las Vegas! Elvis Presley—the King, "old swivel hips," Mr. Las Vegas—makes his debut at the New Frontier. As time passes, Elvis becomes more and more a part of the Las Vegas lore, and his costumes become almost as glitzy as the town itself. While Frankie and Dino and Sammy and the other Rat Pack members may have owned the town for a short while, Elvis transcends it, becoming the divinity that watches over all. In fact, there are still more Elvis impersonators in Vegas (and the world) than any other singer-celebrity. And, of course, Elvis is still alive, isn't he?

[28.] 1956: Roger Baldwin, Wilbert E. Cantey, Herbert Maisel, and James P. McDermott publish "The Optimum Strategy in Blackjack" in the *Journal of the American Statistical Association*. A breakthrough paper, this contains the first Basic Strategy for the game of blackjack and becomes the foundation for all basic strategies that are to follow. It garners very little attention at the time of its publication. However, as a butterfly flapping its wings can ultimately cause a hurricane to develop, this paper becomes the launching pad for the first serious and sustained attack by players on a casino game that can yield the players a mathematical edge.

[29.] 1957: Gamblers Anonymous is founded to help those with gambling problems. Today this organization has chapters throughout the country. Some casino aficionados are resentful of GA because they mistakenly think that GA unnecessarily highlights the evils of gambling. There are no evils to gambling—it is a morally neutral activity—but there are evils when individuals cannot control themselves and subsequently ruin their lives through an addiction. For the overwhelming majority of casino players who enjoy gambling as a hobby, and to the 1,100 players who actually can make long-term profits from casino gambling, Gamblers Anonymous speaks not. But to the individuals who are out of control, GA offers the hand of friendship and self-help.

[30.] 1959: The number 10 hits six times in a row at roulette at the El San Juan Hotel in Puerto Rico. What are the odds of the 10 hitting six times in a row? The odds of this happening are 3,010,936,383 to 1! Place your bets.

[31.] 1959: Baccarat is introduced into American casinos for the first time at the Dunes in Las Vegas. The very first night, gamblers wager with money, not chips, and the house loses a quarter of a million dollars. Baccarat becomes the ultimate high-roller game with millions being won and lost—often within minutes!

[32.] 1960: "The Summit at the Sands" sees Frank Sinatra and the Rat Pack (Sammy Davis Jr., Dean Martin, Joey Bishop, and Peter Lawford) take Las Vegas by storm. This three-week event takes place from January 26 to February 16 just as the movie *Oceans Eleven,* about a daring casino-hotel robbery starring the same Rat Pack, is filmed during the day. Solidifies the Sands as the center of action in the new, swinging Las Vegas.

[33.] 1961: *Scarne's Complete Guide to Gambling* is published. It becomes a prototype for the "all-inclusive" gambling books to come.

[34.] 1962: Jules (Big Julie) Weintraub organizes the first junkets for high rollers to Las Vegas. From this date through 1983, Big Julie brings in some of the biggest gamblers to the Dunes Hotel Casino. Some sources estimate that he is responsible for bringing in close to a half billion dollars in casino revenues to the city.

[35.] 1962: Edward O. Thorp's *Beat the Dealer: A Winning Strategy for the Game of 21* is published. This book launches the card-counting revolution, as it offers a method that can actually change the mathematical expectation of blackjack to favor the player. While complicated and difficult to play, Thorp's early system of card counting sends chills running up and down the spines of casino executives. They have visions of millions of card counters descending on their casinos and wiping them out. Thorp's book actually causes the panicky casinos to change their rules of play, which begins to hurt the bottom line more than a battalion of card counters, as regular players shun the new and "improved" game. The casinos soon revert to their former rules and, with the exception of adding more decks, still offer blackjack games that can be beaten by card counters.

[36.] 1963: Bally's introduces its first electro-mechanical slot machine, the Money Honey. This machine has several revolutionary features, including the first large hopper payout unit that can hold 2,500 coins. Bally's soon takes over as the number one slot machine developer and marketer of slots in the world.

[37.] 1964: John and Edna Luckman found the Gambler's Book Shop (also known as the Gambler's Book Club). This is the first bookstore devoted exclusively to the gambler. It continues in operation at 630 South 11th Street, Las Vegas, NV 89101. It has thousands of books, new, used, and collector's editions, on all forms of gambling. Contains a Gambling Hall of Fame that is a must-see attraction. It is the "in" place for authors, experts, players, and pundits to meet.

[38.] 1965: Allan N. Wilson publishes *The Casino Gamblers Guide*. While a mathematically oriented book that covers the most popular casino games of the period, Wilson's enthusiasm for the games comes shining through. The first and best treatment of the games from a mathematical perspective, true, but Wilson is not just a theorist. He is an avid player, and his adventures are enjoyable to read. A classic, sadly, that is out of print.

[39.] 1965: Muhammad Ali knocks out Floyd Patterson at the Sands. In the battle of champions, current champion Muhammad Ali tortures and torments former champion Floyd Patterson and ultimately gains a 12-round TKO when

Patterson cannot continue. Prior to the fight, Patterson had refused to call Ali by his Muslim name, referring to him instead as Cassius Clay, the name Ali was given at birth. This fight is the first of the big heavyweight mega-fights to be hosted by a casino. In the future, Vegas will become the fight capitol of America, supplanting Madison Square Garden in New York. Casinos can afford to pay the fighters incredible purses because big fights attract the high rollers who love action.

[40.] 1966: Caesar's Palace opens its doors. This hotel-casino, conceived and executed by Jay Sarno, ushers in the age of elegance, luxury, and extravagance surrounding a theme of Roman decadence. (Sarno would later create Circus Circus, the first theme casino with children in mind.) Until this time, most casino "themes" were Western. Even at the end of the 20th century, in an age of mega-resorts, Caesar's Palace is still synonymous with luxury and the high-rolling life.

[41.] 1966: Riverside Casino opens in Laughlin, Nevada, on the Colorado River. Laughlin ultimately will become the fourth casino destination in Nevada, behind Las Vegas, Reno, and Lake Tahoe. Laughlin will cater to the low rollers who are legion by the 20th century's end.

[42.] 1967: Inventor and billionaire Howard Hughes goes on a Las Vegas buying spree. In a short period of time, he buys seven Las Vegas properties. Why? Mr. Hughes "retires" to the penthouse on the 15th floor of the Desert Inn in 1966, where he refuses to be budged by management. When management makes it quite clear that they want the reclusive Mr. Hughes to hit the road, Howard makes them an offer they cannot refuse—he buys the hotel for $14,000,000—twice what it is worth at the time. From that day on, he lives like a hermit in a fastidiously clean luxury cave at the top of the Desert Inn in the midst of the most dynamic and action-packed city in the world. Unfortunately, lucky in business but unlucky in the casino business, Howard Hughes's management team has very little familiarity with the day-to-day workings of a casino, and his Desert Inn does not do the business it should. Nor does the Sands, another Hughes investment. However, Las Vegas's city fathers (and mothers) welcome Hughes with open arms, as he represents a wonderful change from the mob-controlled casinos. In fact, Hughes's arrival is considered a major turning point in Vegas history. Once he enters the picture, other large corporations will begin to look at Nevada as a legitimate area for investment. The only folks not overjoyed with Hughes's arrival are the managers of the Teamsters Pension Funds, who have a lock on Las Vegas casino investments until Hughes comes along.

[43.] 1967–1968: In 1967, Bally introduces the first five-coin multiplier machines, and a year later the company introduces the first three-line machine. These become the standard for slots from this point on.

[44.] 1969: Lawrence Revere publishes *Playing Blackjack as a Business*. Revere's book offers an easy-to-learn and easy-to-use, simplified card-counting system. Revere is responsible for ushering in the age of "simple" counts, accessible to the average, though disciplined, player. This book creates a blackjack playing and publishing boom that continues to this day. Although some current authorities quibble with Revere's estimate of a player's edge over the casinos, most agree that Revere is to Thorp what St. Paul is to Jesus—the herald that brings Thorp's message, in simplified form, to the masses! Revere himself is something of a legend in Las Vegas circles. His other name was Spec Parsons. Now, *that* was a great name for a Las Vegas gambler!

[45.] 1969: Peter Griffin publishes *Theory of Blackjack.* Unlike any previous book on the subject, Griffin thoroughly explores the math behind the game of blackjack, but in a way many non-mathematicians could at least attempt to understand. Griffin is an accomplished blackjack theorist, perhaps the best theorist ever, but he is also an accomplished writer and a great player who could keep track of every single card in the deck. This book is still in print in its ninth edition.

[46.] 1969: The first World Series of Poker is held at the Riverside Casino in Reno, Nevada. It is the brainchild of Tom Morehead.

[47.] 1970: Binion's Horseshoe takes over the World Series of Poker and holds the first *annual* World Series of Poker, which is won by Johnny Moss. This is indicative of the flow of events, as Las Vegas supplants Reno as the number one gambling destination in America. The World Series of Poker is now a major national event as it is televised on cable stations across the country.

[48.] 1970: Dale Electronics introduces the "Poker-Matic" draw poker machine to casinos. This early "TV" machine anticipates the exciting developments in the world of video poker.

[49.] 1971: Dr. Richard Jarecki wins approximately $1,280,000 at roulette from casinos in Monte Carlo and San Remo. Dr. Jarecki is a biased-wheel player who boasts that a giant computer at London University has given him the edge. At the time, no one believes a computer can do such things. In fact, they cannot. Jarecki's story was simply a ruse to allow him to keep playing.

[50.] 1975: The first "video" slot machine debuts, created by the Fortune Coin Company. Computer chips and RNGs will begin to dominate the slot machine market. Today, just about every machine found in just about every casino is a computerized machine that uses a Random Number Generator to select the symbols that will appear on the reels or as cards that will appear on the screen.

[51.] 1975: The Union Plaza in downtown Las Vegas opens the first modern sports book inside a casino. Bob Martin is the odds maker. Later that same year, the Stardust opens its sports book.

[52.] 1976: Bally's introduces a Video Draw Poker machine.

[53.] 1976: New Jersey legalizes casino gambling for Atlantic City. For years the New Jersey legislature debates the idea of legalizing casino gambling in the rapidly deteriorating Atlantic City. Every year, the bill is defeated. Finally, with the Queen of

Resorts looking more like a decaying drag queen on a bad hair day, the legislature relents and allows gaming in Atlantic City. Is a makeover for the Queen in the cards? You bet.

[54.] 1977: Ken Uston and Roger Rapaport publish *The Big Player*. A phenomenally popular book at the time of its publication, this book chronicles the exciting and true adventures of Ken Uston in the casinos and brings the concept of "team play" to the public consciousness for the first time. Here is a sample of how a team can work. A group of blackjack players will enter a casino. Relatively small stakes players will take seats at various tables and count the cards and play the hands according to basic strategy. When the shoe becomes favorable to the player, a small-stakes player will signal the "big player" to jump into the game and make large bets, often table maximum bets of $500 to $2,000. When the shoe becomes unfavorable, the big player (also known as the BP) will leave the table and "wander" around the casino waiting for the next signal from another small-stakes player at another table. It is a remarkably effective system that garners Uston's teams over five million dollars in profit—until the casinos catch on. Because of this and other high-profile blackjack activities, Ken Uston becomes the most famous blackjack player of all time, and his adventures are still the stuff of legend. He goes on to write several other popular blackjack books as well, including *Million Dollar Blackjack* and *Ken Uston on Blackjack*. *The Big Player* is out of print.

[55.] 1977: *Gambling Times* magazine makes its debut. Stanley Sludikoff, also known as blackjack expert Stanley Roberts, assembles a first-rate cadre of gaming writers including Ken Uston, Julian Braun, and Edward O. Thorp, and launches the first popular, slick, national gaming magazine. Changes its name to *Win* magazine in the 1990s and loses its subscription base.

[56.] 1978: Doyle Brunson publishes *Super System: How I Made Over $1,000,000 Playing Poker*. This book is considered by poker aficionados as one of the best poker books of all time.

Brunson is a World Champion and a legendary high-stakes Las Vegas poker icon. He marshals the knowledge of many of poker's top experts for this comprehensive analysis of the game. Still in print in a new edition.

[57.] 1978: Resorts International Hotel Casino opens in Atlantic City. It is characterized by long lines on weekdays, weekend lines that stretch almost a mile down the boardwalk, people packed in like sardines, players six deep waiting for a chance to play blackjack and slots—but it is the herald that sounds the clarion call that the national gambling explosion is about to begin with Resorts as the spark.

[58.] 1978: The first major tournament in blackjack is played at the Sahara Hotel in Las Vegas. Sponsored by an organization called "The World Championship of Blackjack," the tournament is the brainchild of Ed Fishman and offers $250,000 in total prize money with $75,000 going to the eventual winner. Over the years, blackjack tournaments are held successfully at many properties and become an added incentive for players to patronize the casinos that offer them.

[59.] 1979: IGT (International Game Technology) introduces its "Draw Poker" machine, which becomes the standard for machines of this type. Draw poker machines are not like slot machines because skilled players can make choices that reduce the house edge, whereas unskilled players can increase the house edge based on how they play their hands. This skill aspect of video poker will be the reason for the explosion of video poker play that we saw at the end of the 20th century. In fact, some video poker machines can yield a player a positive expectation—if the player plays the right strategy.

[60.] 1980: The devastating MGM Grand fire occurs. On the morning of November 21, 1980, 84 people die (some accounts say 85) and 679 are injured in the biggest casino-hotel fire in American history. Three months later, in February 1981, the Las Vegas Hilton has a fire that kills eight people and injures more than six hundred. These two fires are largely responsible for the *Hotel and Motel Fire Safety Act of 1990*, which requires all hotel and motel rooms and halls to have automatic sprinkler systems and emergency plans posted. The report of the MGM Grand fire states that had the hotel installed automatic sprinklers the fire would have simply caused the sprinklers to cause some water damage due to a "puddle" in the hallway. One odd fact concerning the MGM fire is that many gamblers refused to leave the games in the casino and had to be ordered out of the building! The MGM Grand is now Bally's.

[61.] *circa* 1980: The "suitcase man" arrives at Binion's to make his big bet (see chapter 13).

[62.] 1981: Blackjack expert Arnold Snyder starts *Blackjack Forum* magazine. Still publishing, this magazine is the quarterly bible for serious card counters, as it looks at all aspects of the blackjack wars in both a mathematical and a practical way. Contains lists of blackjack conditions from around the world, reports from experts in the field, and esoteric, as well as practical, analyses of various aspects of the game and some very fine writing as well.

[63.] 1982: The first "slot club" opens in Atlantic City at The Golden Nugget which then becomes Bally's Grand then The Grand and is now the Hilton. But what's in a name? Slot clubs become the rage in the 1990s—even having books written about them.

[64.] 1982: Ken Uston wins his lawsuit against Atlantic City's Resorts International Hotel Casino. The Appellate Division of the New Jersey Superior Court rules that Atlantic City Casinos cannot bar skilled players from their blackjack tables. Uston was banned from playing in 1979, and he challenged the casino's right to bar him based on his ability to count cards, claiming it is a form of discrimination to ban someone because he can think. Although he wins the battle, Atlantic City casinos ultimately win the war, as they quickly institute eight-deck games with poor penetration and countermeasures such as shuffling up and limiting what an individual player can bet. Joseph Campione will challenge these counter measures in the 1990s. Campione will win his case as well, but ultimately the casinos defeat Campione on appeal. As I write this, Atlantic City casinos are allowed by law to offer "selectively" unfavorable conditions for blackjack card counters (limiting minimum to maximum bets, limiting number of hands that can be played, etc.), while offering more favorable conditions for non-counting players—at the same table!

[65.] 1984: The "virtual stop" is created. Mr. Inge Telnaes receives patent 4,448,419 on May 15, 1984, and the world of slot machines will never be the same again. The title of the patent is "Electronic Gaming Device Utilizing a Random Number Generator for Selecting the Reel Stop Positions." It's a mouthful, but it creates the potential for the giant jackpot games to follow. Prior to Telnaes, slots have to have four or more reels in order to have high jackpots. Players intuitively know that getting four jackpot symbols is less likely than getting three, so casinos are looking for some way to *decrease* the probability of hitting the jackpot from what it appears to be without *revealing* that the probability has actually been decreased. Another way to decrease the probability is to make the physical reel larger. At this time, IGT has also been working on a machine with huge reels to increase payouts but decrease a player's probability of hitting them. This concept is not practical because every machine would need to be a Big Bertha.

Perhaps the most important innovation since Fey's Liberty Bell slot was invented, Telnaes patents the idea of making a reel appear to have more stops than it really has. Here is how he put it: "It should be noted that the market demands higher and higher payoffs to maintain and increase player appeal, yet the casino or operator must be assured that the probability of win and payout allows for a reasonable business profit. . . . It is therefore the purpose of this invention to increase the capability of the designer to include high pay-offs without increased physical size of the machine. . . . It should be noted that the players perceive larger machines as being less 'good' in terms of winning and payout chances. That is, large physical machines and a large number of reels develop an attitude in the player which affects the play and acceptance of the machine, although this does not always coincide with the true mathematical reality and probability of payout of the machine . . . this attitude may be more influen-tial on whether or not the machine is played than published figures showing the payoff odds. Thus, it is important to make a machine that is perceived to present greater chances of payoff than it actually has within the legal limitations that games of chance must operate." Telnaes might not win writ-ing awards, but the slot manufacturers have given him the Nobel Prize for Creativity. Without him, many of the newest and most popular machines would have been impossibilities.

[66.] 1984: Frank Sinatra and Dean Martin cause a huge ruckus at the Golden Nugget in Atlantic City. They insist that the blackjack dealer deal the cards from her hands and not use a shoe as is required by the New Jersey state law. After much badgering and verbal abuse, the dealer relents and deals the cards by hand. The Golden Nugget is subsequently fined $25,000, the dealer is sacked, and Sinatra, in a fit of pique, declares he will never perform in New Jersey again. However, the lure of the shore—and the big money from all the whales that attend his concerts—salves his wounded ego, and he returns to perform many concerts at the Sands. Shortly thereafter, Steve Wynn sells the Golden Nugget and vows he is never coming back to Jersey either. No one knows what happened to the poor dealer.

[67.] 1984: Mike Caro publishes *Mike Caro's Book of Tells: The Body Language of Poker*. While most poker books concentrate on the math of the game and reading your cards right, Caro's book explains how to read the people against whom you are playing. A seminal work on the human side of poker—and why are your eyebrows knitting up like that? Do you have a good hand?

[68.] 1984: Luddites beware! Slot machine revenues outpace table games for the first time in recorded history. Yes, this is the year that the slots become king in Nevada and at the Queen of Resorts, Atlantic City. As the century closes, slots account for between 65 and 90 percent of casino revenue, depending on the casino and the venue.

[69.] 1985: Nevada outlaws "devices" (including concealed computers) that previously had been legal. The perfect basic strategy in blackjack is to count every card that comes out of the deck or shoe, weigh it based on its real mathematical effects on the remaining cards in the deck or shoe, and then bet accordingly. No human can do the math fast enough. But computers can. And, in fact, the redoubtable Ken Uston (and others) took such computers into the casinos and began using them. However, once Nevada Governor Richard Bryan signs into law Senate Bill #467 which becomes effective on July 1, 1985, it becomes a felony violation of the cheating statutes for any person in a casino "to use or possess with intent to use any device" which would assist in "projecting the outcome" of a game, "keeping track of the cards played" in a game, "analyzing the probability of the occurrence of an event" related to a game, or "analyzing the strategy for playing or betting" to be used in a game. Though many legal experts believe the anti-device law to be unconstitutionally vague (because card counting itself could be considered a "device," as could a pencil and paper used to keep track of results at baccarat or roulette, let alone simple pocket calculators used in making decisions at the sports book), the law has been copied verbatim into the gaming regulations of many other states.

[70.] 1986: Thomas A. Bass publishes *The Eudemonic Pie*. Can a team of computer geeks beat the roulette wheels in Las Vegas? Yes, they can. Recounts the stirring adventures of a group of young men who employ one of the first computer tracking devices against the roulette wheel. Bass's roulette team is one of the reasons that "devices" are banned. Out of print.

[71.] 1986–1987: IGT introduces Megabucks in 1986, the first multi-casino linked one-dollar progressive slot machine. The first jackpot starts at one million dollars. This ushers in the era of huge jackpots. As revealed by John Robison in the summer 1999 issue of *The New Chance and Circumstance* magazine, the odds of hitting the Megabucks jackpot are 49,846,031 to 1! On February 1, 1987, Terry Williams becomes the first person to win the Megabucks jackpot. He does so at Harrah's in Reno. He wins $4,988,842.14. In the shortest month of the year, Terry wins the biggest jackpot up to that time, with the longest odds of any bet in the casino. That's the long and the short of it!

[72.] 1986–1989 Billy Walter's roulette teams win approximately $4,810,000 from casinos in Las Vegas and Atlantic City. Walter's teams look for biased wheels and when they find them—*wham!*

[73.] 1988: Indian Gaming Act allows Native Americans to operate casinos on their reservations. While some individuals might think that gambling will be a new venture for the Native Americans, in fact native tribes have a long tradition of gambling games and now will be allowed to reinstitute this very important cultural activity. Who said cultural activities have to be boring?

[74.] 1988: Caribbean Stud is brought over from the islands and cruise ships to American casinos by Progressive Games, Inc. Caribbean Stud is now one of the "new" games that seems to have established a permanent niche in the table-game hierarchy, perhaps owing to the fact that players can win rather large sums on select hands, much like slot players can win large sums on select symbols.

[75.] 1988: The Casino Journal Group founds *Casino Player* magazine. The magazine began as a tabloid to be found in Atlantic City hotel rooms. With smart marketing to players of all levels, good writing, and colorful layouts, *Casino Player* becomes the dominant gaming magazine in the country.

[76.] 1989: The King's Club in Brimley, Michigan, opens its doors. It is the first Native American gambling club to offer slots and blackjack games, as opposed to bingo. The Indian casino explosion is about to begin.

[77.] 1989–1990: Iowa, Illinois, and Mississippi legalize gambling on riverboats (or on the water). Most of the riverboats do not actually go on the rivers; they just sit there at dockside or move a few yards offshore and tread water. Many of the other dockside casinos are on mud holes, some dry as a bone, but, hey, who cares? No one is going fishing and the national gambling explosion is on!

[78.] 1991: *Beat the Craps Out of the Casinos: How to Play Craps and Win!* by Frank Scoblete is published. This number one bestselling gaming book since its publication introduces the Captain, a legendary Atlantic City craps player and the originator of the *5-Count*, a system for reducing risk and positioning players to take advantage of hot rolls. The first time in print that anyone discussed the concept of "rhythmic rolling" or precision shooting.

[79.] 1991: The Maxim deals its "dream" blackjack game for three months. From July through September, the Maxim Casino Hotel in Las Vegas deals the best single-deck blackjack game the world has ever seen since card counting came on the scene (and maybe even before that!). With the exception of the burn card, every card is dealt out. If the dealer runs out of cards in mid-round, he just takes the discards, shuffles them and continues dealing. Makes a little known aspect of blackjack strategy—called "end play"—pivotal. The rules are out of this world, too: dealer stands on soft 17; the players can double down on any first two cards; the players can split and re-split pairs, including Aces, and the casino tolerates wide betting spreads. To add icing to an already incredible cake, if a player gets a blackjack (which pays 3 to 2, not even money as some sucker "we deal all cards to the bottom" single-deck games do) with a $5 or more bet, he gets a one-dollar coupon good for one *real* dollar's worth of food or merchandise at any Maxim outlet. Four tables are open for this single-deck game every day, and many of blackjack's greatest players show up to play it. Interestingly enough, the Maxim has many players playing all the blackjack games offered, the casino is doing brisk business at almost all hours of the day and night—even at their six-deck shoes. Seems the atmosphere is so super-charged that even those players who are not skilled are enjoying the adrenaline high of a blackjack paradise and playing it up. Personally, I played the Maxim game for eight weeks and mourn its passing more than the passing of my first pet, a cat named Cat.

[80.] 1992–1993: Lenny Frome publishes *Video Poker: America's National Game of Chance* with Marilyn Guberman, which is the first video poker book based on accurate mathematical calculations to gain a widespread audience. He follows this up with *Winning Strategies for Video Poker*, which gives complete strategies for a host of the most popular video poker games. A former engineer, Frome is the first writer of note to offer mathematically based basic strategies, some of which yield the player a positive expectation. Frome is considered the father of modern video poker strategy.

[81.] 1992: Shuffle Master Gaming introduces the first automatic single-deck shuffling machine and several other companies follow suit. However, in 1993, a team of blackjack advantage players analyzes another company's continuous shuffling machine's operations and devises a method for beating the game of blackjack by tracking the shuffle machine's shuffle. It is back to the drawing board for the executives at Shuffle Master and other manufacturers in order to prevent traceable shuffle-machine shuffles.

[82.] 1992–1993: Greek immigrant Archie Karas has one of the greatest runs in Vegas history (see chapter 13).

[83.] 1993: The casino domino effect hits Canada, and, in short order, the provinces of Ontario and Quebec legalize and open casinos.

[84.] 1993: Shuffle Master Gaming introduces Let It Ride. This game becomes the second most popular table card game after blackjack in the casinos. It offers big payouts, relatively low minimums, and a chance to exercise some strategy decisions that actually increase or decrease the house's edge on the player.

[85.] 1994: Slots are legalized at racetracks in Iowa and Delaware, making racetracks "slot casinos" or "racinos." Do the one-armed bandits help the bottom line? Absolutely. In Iowa, the Prairie Meadows Race Track in Altoona makes one million dollars in its first weekend of slot operations. It was in bankruptcy and restructuring since 1991 when it lost $5.24 million in one year! At Delaware Park racetrack, the total handle for the first year of slot machines is a staggering, record-breaking $91 million. The casino revenue king, slots, saves the sport of kings, horse racing. Machines replace animals to generate income for man . . . hmm, that is the way non-gaming history goes, too, right?

[86.] 1994: David Sklansky publishes *The Theory of Poker.* Many poker players feel that this is the one must-read poker book for the serious player. Covers just about every casino poker game.

[87.] 1994: Shuffle Master introduces its multi-deck shuffler machines. These can now be found in just about every major casino in the United States. By not having human dealers shuffle, the casino saves downtime and increases the number of hands played per hour. That translates into more money for the house.

[88.] 1994: The Foxwoods Resort Casino opens in Connecticut. Not only does Foxwoods become the largest hotel-casino complex owned and operated by American Indians (the

Mashantucket Pequot Tribe), it becomes the largest casino-hotel complex in the world!

[89.] 1994: Frank Sinatra gives his final performance in Las Vegas at the MGM Grand. The era of the Rat Pack has long been finished and now its leader is too.

[90.] 1994: *Break the One-Armed Bandits!* by Frank Scoblete is published. The first book that explains—from an inside source—the actual slot-placement philosophy of the casinos and debunks many of the popular myths surrounding the slot machines. Explains clearly for the non-experts how the modern computer-generated slots and the RNG work.

[91.] 1995: "The Million-Dollar Bum" goes on a tear at Treasure Island in Las Vegas (see chapter 13).

[92.] 1995: The first gaming exposition for players is held in a casino. *Casino Player* magazine holds its first Gaming Festival on September 16 and 17 at the Taj Mahal in Atlantic City. For the first time in history, gambling's greatest authors, personalities, and theorists give seminars and sell their products inside a casino-hotel. Such gaming luminaries as Mike Caro, Anthony Curtis, Bradley Davis, Lenny Del Genio, Lenny Frome, Jim Hildebrand, Jimmy "the Scot" Jordan, Marvin B. Roffman, Paul Rubalcaba, Max Rubin, Frank Scoblete, Arnold Snyder, and Stanford Wong are in attendance. Blackjack guru Snyder is overheard saying: "I never thought in my wildest dreams that I'd ever see a time when *Blackjack Forum* was being sold in a casino!"

[93.] 1996: Stanford Wong opens his Blackjack Page (*www.bj21.com*) on the World Wide Web. It soon becomes the hottest site for discussions of blackjack strategies and analysis on the Internet.

[94.] 1997: Olaf Vancura and Ken Fuchs publish *Knock-Out Blackjack!* This is the first book in 30 years to offer a simplified, but extremely powerful, card-counting system at blackjack, and it causes many card counters to switch from the count systems they have been using. What makes KO revolutionary is its ease of use in both single and multiple-deck games, as there is no need to convert from the running count to the true count.

[95.] 1997: Mike Tyson bites Evander Holyfield during a championship fight and a riot ensues (see chapter 13).

[96.] 1997: Australian billionaire Kerry Packer wins $20 million over several days at MGM Grand in Las Vegas, and several casino executives get the axe for reeling in this big whale who sinks their quarterly earnings report. Or he wins $30 million with the same axing and red ink taking place. Or he wins $40 million and Paul Bunyon's axe cleaves the careers of several cringing casino ex-execs and the red ink flows like blood in the movie *Jaws*. Take your pick because all kinds of stories are making the rounds on this one, but one thing is certain: something big and Bunyonesque went down at the MGM (see chapter 13).

[97.] 1998: The world's largest slot jackpot of the 20th century is won, $27,582,539, on a Megabucks machine at the Palace Station Hotel and Casino in Las Vegas. The date is Sunday, November 15. The winner requests anonymity. You can understand why. She probably does not want anyone touching her to rub some of her luck off. A month previous, this same woman, a retired flight attendant in her mid-60s, had hit for more than $680,000 on the Wheel of Fortune at the same casino. Who says luck doesn't run in streaks? If you are counting, this particular jackpot is the 47th Megabucks to be won in Nevada since its inception in 1986 (the 48th and second biggest jackpot ever, 21.35 million dollars, was won in June of 1999). How many Megabucks jackpots have been won across the country since 1986? About 120 hopefully happy millionaires have shared a total of approximately $500 million.

[98.] 1999: Bellagio opens. Steve Wynn raises the bar for elegance and tone by opening what many people consider to be the best casino-hotel in the world. Unfortunately for Mr. Wynn, one Charles Lund figures out a way to get an edge on some Bellagio slot machines! Lund becomes the first non-cheating *slot* player to be barred from a casino! The high-end openings continue. In quick succession Mandalay Bay, the Venetian, and Paris join the Vegas skyline, while the Resort at Summerlin brings glamor to the outback of Nevada, and Beau Rivage dazzles the folks in Biloxi. The new casino thinking is that people will come to high-end places and spend big money, not necessarily at gambling, but at shops and restaurants and shows, as they do in "real" resort towns.

[99.] 1999: Dice games are legalized in the province of Ontario. It is the first time that dice games are played (legally) in Canada since they were outlawed by Queen Victoria.

[100.] 1999: The National Gambling Impact Study is released. It recommends that the spread of casino gambling be stopped and that a moratorium on all new casino initiatives be put into effect immediately. It also recommends that college sports betting be outlawed in every state including Nevada. The only "pro-player" recommendations made by this antigambling committee are that casinos should post the true odds that the players face in each and every game and on each and every machine. The century opened with the anti-booze and antigambling forces storming the gates, it closes with the antigambling forces pushing for some form of prohibition again. As of the publication of this book, the report has been ignored and more casino venues are in the process of opening.

[101.] 2000: On January 27, the largest jackpot ever recorded, a $34,955,489.56 Megabucks jackpot, was won by Cynthia Jay at The Desert Inn.

[102.] 2001: The first Global Gaming Expo, or G2E, is held at the Las Vegas convention center. Organized by the American Gaming Association, G2E brings together the largest number of casino policy makers and manufacturers.

[103.] 2002: The very first "controlled shooter" craps confer-
ence is held in Las Vegas on September 20, corresponding
with the publication of Sharpshooter's book *Get the Edge at
Craps: How to Control the Dice* and a host of famous "rhythmic
rollers" including Dominator, Mr. Finesse, Bill Burton, Billy
the Kid, Howard "Rock 'n' Roller" Newman, Street Dog,
Sharpshooter, Stickman, Daryl "No Field Five" Henley, and
Randy "Tenor" Rowsey attend. Frank Scoblete is the keynote
speaker. More than 170 "rhythmic rollers" participate. As card
counting was to the 20th century, so will controlled shooting
or "rhythmic rolling" be for the twenty-first century—the
advantage-play method of the most savvy casino players.

I'd like to thank the following individuals, both living and
deceased, and cite the following sources for their help in com-
piling the Most Significant Events in Casino Gambling list: A.
Alvarez (author of *The Biggest Game in Town*); Russell T.
Barnhart (author of *Beating the Wheel*); Bootlegger (gaming
columnist for *www.scoblete.com, The New Chance* and
Circumstance); John Brokopp (gaming columnist for *Daily
Southtown* and *www.scoblete.com*, author of *Thrifty Gambling*
and *Insider's Guide to Internet Gambling*); Bill Burton (author of
Get the Edge at Low-Limit Texas Hold'em and host of *About.com*);
Don Catlin (author of *The Lottery Book: The Truth Behind the
Numbers!* and gaming columnist on *www.scoblete.com*);
Marshall Fey (author of *Slot Machines: A Pictorial History of the
First 100 Years*); Adam Fine (managing editor of *Casino Player*
and *Strictly Slots* magazines); the Gamblers Book Club; the
Golden Nugget Web site; John Grochowski (gaming colum-
nist for *www.scoblete.com, Chicago Sun Times*, Midwest Gaming
and Travel, and author of *The Casino Answer Book, The Video
Poker Answer Book, The Craps Answer Book,* and *The Slot
Machine Answer Book*); Russell Guindon (Nevada Gaming
Control Board); Daniel Heneghan (New Jersey Casino
Control Commission); Anthony Holden (author of *Big Deal*);
Indian Gaming Web site; Michael Konik (author of *The Man
with the $100,000 Breasts*); Hotel and Motel Fire Safety Act of

1990; *Las Vegas Review Journal*; *The Las Vegas Sun*; Patricia Marvel (public relations director of Shuffle Master Gaming); John May (gaming columnist for *www.scoblete.com* and author of *Baccarat for the Clueless* and *Get the Edge at Blackjack*); The National Gaming Impact Study (Preliminary Report); Eddie Olsen (editor of *Blackjack Confidential Magazine*); Alene Paone (gaming columnist for *www.scoblete.com*); Christopher Pawlicki (gaming columnist for *Casino.com*, *www.scoblete.com*, and author of *Get the Edge at Roulette*); John Robison (gaming columnist for *Midwest Gaming and Travel* and *Double Down* magazines, contributor to *Casino Player*, *Strictly Slots*, and *Atlantic City Insider* magazines, managing editor of *www.scoblete.com*, *The Slot Expert's Guide to Playing Slots*); Jack Sheehan, (editor of *The Players: The Men Who Made Las Vegas*); Carl Sifakas (author of *The Encyclopedia of Gambling*); Arnold Snyder (editor of *Blackjack Forum* magazine, author of *Blackbelt in Blackjack* and *Blackjack Wisdom*); Rick Sorensen, (public relations director of International Game Technology, IGT); Henry Tamburin (author of six books and three videos on casino gambling, gaming columnist for *Casino Player* and *www.scoblete.com*); Walter Thomason (gaming columnist for *Midwest Gaming and Travel* and *www.scoblete.com*, author of *The Experts' Guide to Casino Games*, *Blackjack for the Clueless*, and *21st Century Blackjack*); William N. Thompson (author of *Legalized Gambling: A Reference Handbook*); Ken Uston (author of *Million Dollar Blackjack*); Barney Vinson (gaming columnist for *Las Vegas Style* and *www.scoblete.com*, author of *Ask Barney* and *The Las Vegas Kid*).

Appendix

Some Recommended Gambling Resources

The following list is not the be-all and end-all of casino gambling books. There are many fine books that I was not able to include because of space limitations or because I have not read them yet. In the interests of humility, I have put my books and tapes at the end in a separate list. On second thought, the heck with humility, I will put mine first!

Books and Tapes by Frank Scoblete

Armada Strategies for Spanish 21 (Bonus Books, $12.95)
Baccarat Battle Book (Bonus Books, $12.95)
Beat the Craps Out of the Casinos: How to Play Craps and Win! (Bonus Books, $9.95)
Best Blackjack (Bonus Books, $14.95)
Bold Card Play: Caribbean Stud, Let It Ride, Three-Card Poker (Bonus Books, $12.95)
Break the One-Armed Bandits! (Bonus Books, $9.95)
Captain's Craps Revolution! (Paone Press, $21.95)

Craps Underground: The Inside Story of How Controlled Shooters Are Winning Millions from the Casinos! (Hardcover, Bonus Books, $24.95)

Forever Craps: The Five-Step Advantage-Play Method! (Bonus Books, $13.95)

Guerrilla Gambling: Beat the Casinos at their Own Games! (Bonus Books, $12.95)

Morons of Blackjack and Other Monsters (Paone Press, $16.95)

Power of Positive Playing (Audio Cassette, Paone Press, $16.95)

Sharpshooter Craps (Audio Cassette, Paone Press, $16.95)

Slot Conquest (Audio Cassette, Paone Press, $16.95)

Spin Roulette Gold: Secrets of Beating the Wheel! (Bonus Books, $14.95)

Victory at Video Poker! with Video Craps, Blackjack and Keno (Bonus Books, $12.95)

Winning Strategies at Blackjack (Video Tape, Goldhil Home Media, $21.95)

Winning Strategies at Craps Video (Video Tape, Goldhil Home Media, $21.95)

Winning Strategies at Slots with Video Poker (Video Tape, Goldhil Home Media, $21.95)

Books by Other Authors

Titles in bold are a part of my "Scoblete Get the Edge Guides" series, or have forewords or chapters in them by me.

General Gambling

The following books deal with more than one game, although not all deal with all the games. Some just deal with "color," or "background." All are worth reading.

109 Ways to Beat the Casino edited by Walter Thomason (Bonus Books, $13.95)

American Casino Guide **edited by Steve Bourie (Casino Vacations, $14.95)**

American Mensa Guide to Casino Gambling by Andrew Brisman (Sterling, $17.95)

Beyond Counting by James Grosjean (RGE, $39.95)

Book Casino Managers Fear the Most by Marvin Karlins (Gollehon, $7.99)

Casino Answer Book **by John Grochowski (Bonus Books, $12.95)**

Casino Gambling: A Winner's Guide by Jerry Patterson, et al (Perigee, $13.95)

Casino Gambling the Smart Way by Andrew N. S. Glazer (Career Press, $14.95)

Casino Secrets by Barney Vinson (Huntington Press, $14.95)

Casino Tournament Strategy by Stanford Wong (Pi Yee Press, $29.95)

Chip-Wrecked in Las Vegas by Barney Vinson (Mead Publishing, $19.95)

Comp City by Max Rubin (Huntington Press, $19.95)

Complete Idiot's Guide to Gambling Like a Pro by Spector and Wong ($18.95)

Encyclopedia of Gambling by Carl Sifakis (Facts on File, $19.95)

Experts' Guide to Casino Games **edited by Walter Thomason (Carol, $16.95)**

Gamblers Digest **edited by Dennis Thornton (Krause Publications, $24.95)**

Frugal Gambler by Jean Scott (Huntington Press, $12.95)

Gambling Wizards by Richard W. Munchkin (Huntington Press, $19.95)

Getting the Best of It by David Sklansky (Two-Plus-Two, $29.95)

Henry Tamburin on Casino Gambling (Research Services Unlimited, $15.95)

Las Vegas Behind the Tables by Barney Vinson (Gollehon Publishing, $6.99)

Pay the Line by John Gollehon (Gollehon Publishing, $5.99)

The Quotable Gambler by Paul Lyons (Lyons Press, $20)

Silberstang's Encyclopedia of Games and Gambling (Cardoza Publishing, $17.95)

Smart Casino Gambling by Olaf Vancura (Index Publishing, $24.95)

Thrifty Gambling by John Brokopp (Bonus Books, $13.95)

Winner's Guide to Casino Gambling by Edwin Silberstang (Signet, $14.95)

Winning at Casino Gambling by Lyle Stuart (Barricade Books, $18)

Baccarat

72 Days at the Baccarat Table by Erick St. Germain (Zumma, $24.95)

Baccarat for the Clueless by John May (Carol Publishing, $12)

Lyle Stuart on Baccarat (Barricade Publishing, $20)

Winning Baccarat Strategies by H. Tamburin and D. Rahm (Research Services, $19.95)

Blackjack

Basic Blackjack by Stanford Wong (Pi Yee Press, $14.95)

Big Player by Ken Uston (Henry Holt, out of print)

Blackbelt in Blackjack by Arnold Snyder (RGE Publishing, $19.95)

Blackjack and the Law by Nelson Rose and Robert Loeb (RGE Publishing, $24.95)

Blackjack Attack by Don Schlesinger (RGE, $19.95)

Blackjack Autumn by Barry Meadows (T. R. Publishing, $14.95)

Blackjack Bluebook by Fred Renzey (Blackjack Mentor, $14)

Blackjack Blueprint: How to Operate a Blackjack Team by Rick Blaine (RGE, $39.95)

Blackjack for Blood by Bryce Carlson (Pi Yee Press, $19.95)

Blackjack: Take the Money and Run! by Henry Tamburin (Research Services, $11.95)

Blackjack Wisdom by Arnold Snyder (RGE, $19.95)

Blackjack Your Way to Riches by Richard Canfield (Lyle Stuart, $14.95)

Blackjack's Winning Formula by Jerry Patterson (Perigee, $9.95)

Burning the Tables in Las Vegas by Ian Andersen (Huntington Press, $27.95)

Bringing Down the House by Ben Mezrich (Free Press, $24)

Fundamentals of Blackjack by Chambliss and Roginski (GBC, $12.95)

Get the Edge at Blackjack by John May (Bonus Books, $13.95)

Ken Uston on Blackjack (Barricade Books, $12.95)

Knock-Out Blackjack by Vancura and Fuchs (Huntington Press, $17.95)

Las Vegas Blackjack Diary by Stuart Perry (RGE, $19.95)

Million Dollar Blackjack by Ken Uston (Carol Publishing, $18.95)

Playing Blackjack as a Business by Lawrence Revere (Lyle Stuart, $16.95)

Professional Blackjack by Stanford Wong (Pi Yee Press, $19.95)

Theory of Blackjack by Peter Griffin (Huntington Press, $12.95)

Twenty-First Century Blackjack by Walter Thomason (Bonus Books, $12.95)

World's Greatest Blackjack Book by Humble and Cooper (Doubleday, $11.95)

Craps

72 Hours at the Craps Table by B. Mickelson ($6.95)

A Guide to Craps Lingo by Fagans and Guzman (Snake Eyes, $9.95)

Craps Answer Book by John Grochowski (Bonus Books, $13.95)

Craps A Smart Shooter's Guide by Thomas Midgley (GBC, $12.95)

Craps System Tester by Erick St. Germain (Zumma, $24.95)

Craps: Take the Money and Run! by Henry Tamburin (Research Services, $11.95)

Dice Control for Casino Craps by Yuri Kononenko (Progress Publishing, $29.95)

Dice Doctor by Sam Grafstein (Casino Press, $19.95)

Get the Edge at Craps: How to Control the Dice by **Sharpshooter (Bonus Books, $14.95)**

Make Your Living Playing Craps by Larry Edell (Leaf Press, $19.95)

Scarne on Dice by John Scarne (Wilshire Books, $20)

Tina Trapp's Guide to Craps by Larry Edell (Leaf Press, $14.95)

Miscellaneous

24/7 Living It Up and Doubling Down in The New Las Vegas by Andres Martinez (Dell Books, $14.95)

77 Ways to Get the Edge at Casino Poker by Fred Renzey (Bonus Books, $14.95)

Art of Gambling Through the Ages by Flowers and Curtis (Huntington Press, $65)

Casino by Nicholas Pileggi (out of print)

Complete Guide to Winning at Keno by David Cowles (Cardoza Publishing, $14.95)

Fly on the Wall: Recollections of Las Vegas' Good Old, Bad Old Days by Dick Odessky (Huntington Press, $14.95)

Get the Edge at Low-Limit Texas Hold'em by Bill Burton (Bonus Books, $14.95)

The Lottery Book: The Truth Behind the Numbers by Don Catlin (Bonus Books, $14.00)

Man with the $100,000 Breasts and Other Stories by Michael Konik (Huntington Press, $24.95)

Mastering the Game of Let It Ride by Stanley Ko ($7.95)

No Limit: The Rise and Fall of Bob Stupak and Las Vegas' Stratosphere Tower by John L. Smith (Huntington Press, $21.95)

Optimal Strategy for Pai Gow Poker by Stanford Wong (Pi Yee Press, $14.95)

Super Casino by Pete Earley (Bantam Books, $7.50)

Telling Lies and Getting Paid by Michael Konik (Huntington Press, $22.95)

Without Reservation: How a Controversial Indian Tribe Rose to Power and Became the World's Largest Casino (Harper Perennial, $14)

Novels

Comped by Bill Kearney (Ian Scott Press, $16.95)
Counter by Kevin Blackwood (Wooden Pagoda Press, $14)
Dice Angel by Brian Rouff (Hardway Press, $14.95)
Fools Die by Mario Puzo (Mass Market, $7.99)

Roulette

Beating the Wheel by Russell Barnhart (Lyle Stuart, $14.95)
Get the Edge at Roulette: How to Predict Where the Ball Will Land by Christopher Pawlicki (Bonus Books, $13.95)
Roulette System Tester by Erick St. Germain (Zumma, $24.95)
Secrets of Winning Roulette by Martin Jenson (Cardoza Publishing, $16.95)

Slot Machines

Robbing the One-Armed Bandits! by Charles Lund (RGE Publishing, $14.95)
Secrets of Modern Slot Playing by Larry Mak (L&M Publications, $9.95)
Slot Expert's Guide to Playing Slots by John Robison (Huntington Press, $6.95)
Slot Machine Answer Book by John Grochowski (Bonus Books, $12.95)
Slot Machine Mania by Dwight and Louise Crevelt (Gollehon, $6.99)

Video Poker

Million Dollar Video Poker by Bob Dancer (Huntington Press, $16.95)
Video Poker Answer Book by John Grochowski (Bonus Books, $13.95)

Video Poker Mania by Dwight Crevelt (Gollehon, $6.99)
Video Poker Optimum Play by Dan Paymar ($19.95)

Index

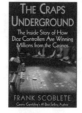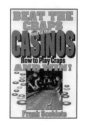